REASON AND BEAUTY
IN THE
POETIC MIND

REASON AND BEAUTY

IN THE

POETIC MIND

BY

CHARLES WILLIAMS

OXFORD
AT THE CLARENDON
1933

PREFACE

THE four corners of this book lie at the following points (i) the use of the word Reason by Wordsworth in the *Prelude*; (ii) the abandonment of the intellect by Keats in the *Nightingale* and the *Urn*; (iii) the emphasis laid on Reason by Milton in *Paradise Lost*; (iv) the schism in Reason studied by Shakespeare in the tragedies. Add to these the four middle points of (i) the definition of Beauty by Marlowe in *Tamburlaine*; (ii) the imagination of it by Keats in the same two odes; (iii) the identification of it with Reason in *Paradise Lost*; (iv) the humanization of it in the women of *Troilus* and *Othello* and the later plays; and the ground plan will be sufficiently marked. The studies are meant as literary, and not as either philosophical or aesthetic criticism. They do not attempt to consider what the poets ought to do, only what they have done, and that from the special point of view of their explicit use of those two words, or of their implicit attention to them.

The book is therefore but an exploration of the content of certain places of poetry, in an order suggested by the relative richness of that content. There are obviously many other places that might be considered, and the present way is open to the objection that it has been chosen to fit a predetermined pattern. Patterns are the bane, as they are the necessity, of criticism as of life; they can be corrected only by destruction, and no doubt this pattern will soon enough be destroyed. But their creation and destruction is our only method; and I am not conscious of having anywhere dishonestly forced an interpretation or ingeniously sought for correspondences. At least this pattern does not go outside the verse; it can therefore be considered and (if desirable) denied by any reader of the verse without expert biographical, historical, or philosophical knowledge.

After a small preliminary discussion the order of the chapters moves from the definitions of Wordsworth and Marlowe through the arguments of Pope, the allegories of Spenser, and the contemplation of Keats, to the division of reason in Shakespeare. The greater achievements of Milton and the later Shakespeare suggest two hemispheres of imagination, and it is with the cartography of those two hemispheres, one inhabited by Reason, the other by Unreason, that the later chapters are concerned. That definition is theirs on their own showing; it is *Paradise Lost* which pretends to deal with Reason, and *Lear* which pretends to deal with Unreason. Even the strongest opposition to the present pattern might admit so much.

The relation between poetic experience and actual experience, which has divided some critics, has been no more than touched on. That relation is of high importance, yet it is obscure. We must not make poetry serve our morals, yet we must not consider it independent of our morals. It is not a spiritual guide, yet it possesses a reality which continually persuades us to repose upon it even in practical things of every day. We have only to enjoy it, but only in proportion as we enjoy it with our whole being can it be said of it that no man shall take its joy from us. But that discussion is beyond the purpose of the present book.

C. W.

CONTENTS

THE OSTENTATION OF VERSE

THE distinction between prose and verse has long been accepted; the distinction between prose and poetry has often been discussed. The two lines of demarcation have not been allowed to coincide. It is a habit of our easier culture to say that poetry can be written in prose, except that since the 'nineties 'prose-poems' have gone a little out of fashion. Passages from Sir Thomas Browne or Traherne or Ruskin are quoted as defining an exaltation which is one with poetic exaltation; and even passages of a less exalted but more simple or tender kind in Hardy or Alice Meynell are gathered under the same heading. 'Poetry can be written in prose'; and only the uneducated childlike mind is allowed to suppose that the pattern of lines makes any difference. None of us are willing to acknowledge ourselves mere babes in culture and therefore we believe all this and repeat it.

Certainly when in years we were children, before we knew that culture existed, we recognized poetry by its lines. A poetry book was one in which the printing did not go straight on, covering the whole page, but stopped short and began again, probably with a capital letter. All printing of that recognizable kind was poetry; we knew nothing of the sad distinction between poetry and verse. But then, as we grew older, they robbed us of our simplicity. There was verse which was not poetry; well, that was, after all, only a difference in quality which the unfortunate young discover to exist—*semper*, *ubique*, *in omnibus*. But then there was prose which was poetry. And that instruction, though no doubt it gave some prose a title to which it had at least a partial claim, left a sadness behind. Poetry was no longer to be known by its lines; the mere magical look of the thing meant nothing. But why then write in lines?

It was discovered, later on, to be more fun, especially if lines (in those far-off days) involved rhymes, and stanzaic arrangements. Also it confined and defined one's impulse, one's labour, and one's result. To write a poem was a more simple and satisfactory thing than to write a piece of prose. There was a reason for writing it, merely because it was complete in itself, a poem. It was also, whether the fact were recognized or not, easier. Prose betrayed us more easily than verse. The lines, the rhymes, the stanzas concealed, by the thrill that their discovery gave us, the lack of any thrill communicated by ourselves. We were astonished, within ourselves, to find that 'adore' and 'more' rhymed in our poem as well as in Lovelace, and that we could provide them with a fresh reason for rhyming. Lovelace had not seen our sunrise or our young lady, and our innocence combined with our ignorance to write verse. But all such reasons did not alter the truth that poetry (they said) could be written in prose, and that the lovely arrangement of lines was a sign of verse, but not of poetry.

words in verse, and prose is power communicated by words not in verse? Have stanzas, couplets, and lines nothing whatever to do with poetry? Or is there something still to be said for maintaining not merely that poetry is and ought to be a word used in opposition to the word prose, but that verse is necessarily a part of poetry and necessarily is not a part of prose?

Verse is a general name given to many different arrangements of single and, in some sense, self-sufficient lines compacted together and related between themselves. Sometimes their relation is further demonstrated by rhyme; sometimes it is not. But it has always been demonstrated by the varying lengths and stresses of the lines. Yes, but prose also is composed of words, variously stressed, arranged in varying lengths. What then is the difference?

The difference would seem to be simple—in verse the reader is deliberately referred to a chosen measure; in prose he is not so referred. That reference —whether it be to the normal decasyllabic line of traditional blank verse, or any one among our innumerable stanzaic forms, or the couplet, or even to a deliberate irregularity—is made known to him by the verse itself, and is ostentatiously insisted on by the verse itself. The ostentation is a part of the verse. It is a necessary part of verse that one line should be a vivid conditioning of the next, and that on arriving at the next, the reader should remain vividly aware of that past power thus conditioning him. But the reader of prose sentences is by no means so memorably conditioned. Or to put it in another way—in reading verse one always refers back sensationally to the preceding line and is aware of that reference ; in prose if one refers it is without so acute an awareness. One is, in prose, conditioned, but one is not by any means so intensely aware of the pattern of that conditioning, of the unit and units of the immediate past, because the variation and relation between the various 'lengths' of the writing is not deliberately ostentatious.

No doubt a reader with sufficiently sensitive ears could follow the relations of all the sentences in *Gulliver's Travels* and could perhaps detect at last a 'basic sentence' on which all the actual sentences are variations. No doubt a less gifted but still sensitive reader would carry in his mind the vibrations of all the sentences in the last page or two of whatever book he was reading, and be wisely aware that they prepared him for the next sentence, and in what relation that next sentence stood to its past. But it might, I think, be allowed that prose does not insist on this reference as verse does ; and that when prose does forget itself and too quickly remind us of its immediate past we consider it as unsatisfactory as we do poetry which does not so remind us. There is not—except for scientists—a continually reimposed unit of sensation in prose ; there is in verse. There is metre—the measurement of that unit—in verse. Identity vehemently exists beneath the variableness of the one, but not of the other.

But what then does this extra quality of verse which may be called the repetition of the pattern, the quality of which the measure is its metre—what does it do for us? It gives us, certainly, an added delight; it is, when it is well done, more fun. *Paradise Lost* is much more fun written in blank verse than it would be in prose, or is so to any one capable of enjoying that particular kind of fun. Let us have all the delights of which we are capable. But is this fun anything more than the artistic ingenuity of Milton in discovering so many variations on his basic line? Yes, it gives us an additional experience, the experience of deliberate choice, imposed upon us, deliberately demanding the assent of our own choice, and ostentatiously reminding us that Milton's harmonization of all his elements is Miltonic and not natural, imperative and not persuasive, the reflection of the limitation of man's nature magnificently worked into the very stuff of the poem. But prose does not so magnificently remind us of man's limitation.

It is an experience of deliberate choice. If a poet writes a poem he discovers and assents to the form that poem is to take. He agrees to a proposal which his mind, or something greater than his mind, makes to him. The agreement is often so delightful and so laborious that the mere fact of agreement is lost in the physic of his pain, in both the pain and the physic. But in effect he determines to know the subject of his poem so, and not otherwise; so— by that particular measurement of discovery and definition. In that effort assuredly the subject changes; it becomes no more the experience of imagined fact, but the poetic result. It abandons actuality for poetry. For, among other reasons, it has absorbed into itself not merely the fact but the poet experiencing the fact, and has made a harmony of both—has indeed made a new thing of both which is to us a new experience[1]. It has therefore taken into itself the nature of the poet and has made that a necessary part of the poem; and this it has done by its rhythms and their metre, its stanzaic form, its rhymes, its diction, and what not. But of all these characteristics the one which most immediately, most swiftly, and most continuously assists that change of subject and imposes the new thing on us is the distinction of the rhythmical form.

Certainly diction has a great deal to do with it, and diction is a great element of prose as well as of poetry. But diction, if it can be called a pattern at all, is a remoter pattern, and less immediately sensational. Form of diction depends for its recognition far more on the reader's chance capacity than does the rhythmical form. Its ostentation and its imposition are more consonant with his own power, the amplitude of his mind (in Wordsworth's phrase). The rhythmical form will no doubt give him additional gratification according as his mind becomes more ample, and may reach states in which a great amplitude is necessary before it can be properly understood. But so long as this rhythmical form divides itself into lines and prints itself so (presumably because of some inner necessity of its nature),

[1] It is therefore extremely uncertain whether any poet ever conveys the emotion he set out to convey, though he is often stated to do merely that. He, as well as the reader, discovers something else in making the poem; he discovers (i) his own method of experiencing, (ii) his own method of communicating that experience. Here are three things that go to make up the result.

so long it makes ostentation a part of its very existence in a way in which prose does not. Prose pretends and tends to subdue its own method of existence
to its business of dealing with the reader, but poetry
desires and determines to subdue the reader to its
own method of existence. It is why we call Swift
good prose, and Milton good poetry.

This ostentation and imposition then, this pattern
of measured arrangement, this conditioning of the
present and the future by the immediate past, this
reference to the identity of a basic fact, is an imperative part of verse, and being the poet's choice conveys
his choice into our experience. It has developed an
element of its style into an ostentation and an imposition, and made it of the first importance to its
own being. There is therefore a limitation of which,
in verse, we are more acutely aware than in the
most exalted—or otherwise effective—prose. The
ostentatious pattern is an expansion and a limitation
at once; it gives us a more complex effect in the
resulting poem, and enables us to realize more
swiftly and fully the fact that this is how the original
subject is being known. It helps therefore the individual effect, and compels us to realize that the
subject has been known in this way. Certainly when
we read the poem we are not allowed so to divide
those effects, for it is neither the pattern nor the
subject of which we are separately aware, but the
resultant whole. But they may be spoken of separately for the purpose of justly apprehending the
whole. And, so speaking, we may understand that
the limitation by the pattern is in itself a further
enlargement, for it gives us—what we may be less

apt to retain in all but very exalted prose—the sense
that things are known by man according to his own
nature. Prose, especially sweet and rational prose,
conceals its human limitations. It may argue or
instruct or exhort, but all that while it subdues or
hides from us the pattern which is our reminder
that its conclusions are what they are because of its
own limitations—which are its writer's—which are
in the nature of man. Man cannot know things by
any means but through his own nature, and it is
that nature in its thousand different capacities, but
still only man's, which the pattern of poetry makes
ostentatious to us. Let the rhythms be as subtle and
complex and subdued as we will, let the metre be
irregular, let the relation of the lines be violent or
harsh, let silence or clangour be part of that relation, still in any piece of writing which is meant to
be read as verse rather than prose, the fact of the
pattern, imposed upon us however gently, ostentatious before us however quietly, presents us in its
very sensation with the ineluctable fact that man
only apprehends his experiences according to his
own nature. It refers us continually back to its unit,
and its unit is the decision of its writer. It is that
fact which poetry willingly embraces; and that from
which prose, as it were, turns away. Therefore when
the direct metre of verse appears in the midst of the
indirect metre of prose, when a prose paragraph
breaks into blank verse, we feel the intrusion un-
desirable, for we are violently reminded of what we
have been encouraged to forget.

   It is true that, though the pattern thus recalls us
to the individual choice, it makes that choice in

turn impersonal. The patterns of our English verse have been often—too often—repeated; it may be that our frailty is by now weary of them for a century or so. But while they existed they imposed themselves on us as something more impersonal than any movement of prose, at the same time that their mere adoption reminded us of the personal decision. The sonnet is an example. To read those arrayed rhymes, with the octave and sestet, is to be intensely aware that some particular thing exists so, and that the arrangement, which is non-rational, is a necessary part of that thing. It is a personal choice among impersonal patterns, and both adjectives impose upon us their corresponding qualities. In both the effect differs from prose, for in prose those qualities are derived from our reading instead of being known as a primary condition of our reading.

It might therefore be possible to use the words *poetic* and *prosaic* with a definite intention of separating two methods of writing of which the one does and the other does not ostentatiously insist on a certain fact in the nature of writing itself, and therefore in the nature of experience itself. In that sense a poem would reasonably be regarded, as in fact we have tended to regard it, as a greater thing than a piece of prose—other facts being equal. For it is precisely a fuller experience ; it takes man's limitation and makes that explicitly a part of his total sensation. It avoids the last illusion of prose, which so gently sometimes and at others so passionately pretends that things are thus and thus. In poetry they also are thus and thus, but because the arrangement of the lines, the pattern within the whole, will have it so; the magnificence of its assertion is made magnificent by its own limitation, and we know at once what we know, how we know it, and that we cannot know it outside our own nature, which in our lives is the thing that makes a pattern of our experience. In life it is no doubt wise to be very careful that we do not attempt to impose too easy and repetitive a pattern on the vast of experience. But we cannot avoid beginning with some kind of pattern, however we vary and alter it, otherwise we should not know anything. So in art we proceed from flagrancy to subtlety. But in poetry through all the subtlety the flagrancy remains. Exquisitely leaning to an implied untruth, prose persuades us that we can trust our natures to know things as they are; ostentatiously faithful to its own nature, poetry assures us that we cannot— we know only as we can. If indeed we choose to believe that great poetry is in some incomprehensible sense native to the universe, that its justice is more accurate than that of prose, and more consistent with the things of which we only know that we know them so—that is our personal decision, and in effect a non-poetic decision: that is, it has nothing to do with the poetic genius. It may be more or less or equally important, but it is not the same. We cannot say that poetry is true except in the sense that we say that love or religion or any philosophy is true. But we can say that in its fullness there is no mightier experience—and few as mighty—known to man.

II

There is, it seems, in philosophy, a charming
concept which is called 'the specious present'. It
means that present which is commonly regarded as
the present, being neither the immediate infinitely
passing *now* nor the eternal now; it is the present as
at any particular time considered in relation to the
past and the future; and it may in consequence be
five minutes, or a year, or any longer period, any
period so long as it is conceived as opposed to the
complementary concepts of a past and a future. There
are therefore three presents—the true present, the
specious present, the eternal present.

It is not for these elementary studies to plunge
into philosophy; they do but borrow a likeness. In
man, considered as a subject for poetry, there are
three selves—his immediate self, his specious self,
and his eternal self. Good poetry can be made out
of all these.

Poetry which makes itself out of man's immediate
self is normally—let us be rash and say at once—
lyric: either in actual lyrics or lyrical moments.
It is that poetry which succeeds in turning one
poignant emotion into another poignant emotion,
without introducing any modifying or transmuting
elements, except of course itself.

> I would I were where Helen lies
>   On fair Kirconnell Lea.

> Hame, hame, hame! O hame fain wad I be!

> O dark, dark, dark! amid the blaze of noon.

The tendency of such movements is towards

themselves alone. The poetry is of course complex, however simple, for the reason suggested above: if you take an emotion and express it in a vehement pattern of associative words, you have a different though perhaps allied emotion. 'I would I were where Helen lies' is not the same thing as grief for Helen: it even in a sense contradicts it, for who would want to be where Helen lies while we can enjoy her death so marvellously? Who would wish Milton to see while we can enjoy his blindness so greatly? Or if one does, who does not recognize that he is introducing a non-poetic judgement, and refusing poetry for the sake of sympathy or pity or something equally outside itself? But though the poetic result may be necessarily complex even in its simplest form, yet its subject has been simple, and its effort has been towards a simplicity of its own. It is an effort to catch the sharpest poignancy of some experience, a sharpness which even in life we so often hardly realize. It takes that, it multiplies it by itself, it presents us with another immediate delight. It attempts to take the most immediate self of man and turn it into the most direct poetry.

But, as the immediate present can never be understood, because in being understood it is bound to become the specious present, so the immediate self can hardly ever be used. Poetry takes more frequently as its subject the specious self: the *Ode to a Nightingale* is a great example. There a whole present awareness, intense, but enlarged from the direct moment and emotion, is turned into an enlarged poetic experience. 'Away, away! for I

will fly to thee' images a different kind of present
and of self from 'I would I were where Helen lies'.
It is this kind of poetry which is most common; it
is also this kind of poetry which is apt to become,
in the worst sense, specious poetry. But that fact
does not spoil the real poetry, any more than our
frequent misunderstanding and misuse of the
specious present alters the fact of the specious present. It is this kind of self which offers poetry its
most frequent opportunities. The *Ancient Mariner*,
the *Vanity of Human Wishes*, the *Unknown Eros*, the
Midsummer-Night's Dream, *Comus* are, considered as
whole poems, examples. They may all of them,
sometimes or often, change into an effort at the
simplicity of the immediate self. But as a general
rule the humanity which they transmute contains
space and time within it, and that space and time
are of the nature of the verse.

> Where thou perhaps under the whelming tide
> Visit'st the bottom of the monstrous world.

> I long to talk with some old lover's ghost
> Who died before the god of love was born.

> Will no one tell me what she sings?—
> Perhaps the plaintive numbers flow
> For old, unhappy, far-off things,
> And battles long ago.

> If music be the food of love, play on;
> Give me excess of it, that, surfeiting,
> The appetite may sicken and so die.

> Hope springs eternal in the human breast;
> Man never is, but always to be blest.

> For soul is form and doth the body make.

And so on, and so on. This is the specious self as the subject of poetry.

And the eternal present? or, in the present parallel, the eternal self? Or (may we say?) eternal poetry? That certainly is a different and more difficult thing, since we have not yet discovered any way of writing poetry in time which shall include all the experiences of time—'the perfect and simultaneous possession of everlasting life'. But the greatest poetic experiences are of a nature which include the lesser. They do not explain them philosophically; they relate them poetically. They are in general of two kinds: (i) the complete and complex experience of a great poem—such as *Paradise Lost*, (ii) the lines which, generally but not always, in such poems carry in themselves the sense of much experience known and determined. The nearest we can get to eternity is either all moments or one moment. But then the one moment must, in that aspect, be felt as entirely self-contained; it must definitely not 'look before and after'. Such lines nevertheless may be assisted in their effect by their place in a poem. The last lines of *Paradise Regained*—

> He unobserved
> Home to his mother's house private returned

—have their amazing effect partly by their place. They do not look before, but all that has gone before leads up to and contrasts with that actual fact; in a sense, all *Paradise Regained* does but define that moment. This is the conclusion of the whole matter, but it also contains the whole matter, as, for example, 'who this is we must learn' does not. We have learnt;

we know who the 'He' is, and what 'unobserved' and 'private' imply, and why 'his mother's house' and how 'returned'. All great poetry in a sense is final.

> My desolation doth begin to make
> A better life,

is as complete as

> I'll be your wife if you will marry me;
> If not I'll die your maid, to be your fellow
> You may deny me, but I'll be your servant
> Whether you will or no.

Both of these moments are perfect; both yet look forward to some other moment. It is their nature to do so; to be complete with the awareness of something else. But the second gathers up that future and defines it and brings it back into itself, so that we feel that that defined future does but help *now* to define the moment. The kind of betterness which it foresees over the past is explained. This is Miranda absolutely aware of herself and what she will be.

> Warring in heaven against heaven's matchless king—

is another example. A complete and obstinate futility is perfectly expressed; all the future is defined in 'matchless', all the insanity in 'in heaven against heaven's . . . king'. It is Satan absolutely aware of his own act, and all the rest of the celestial war does but expand and explain it. Such lines certainly are not to be called eternal. But they are of a greater nature than the lines which go to and fro in the specious self, for they define that whole self. They define it according to the way in which the poet chooses to know it: that is, they refer to no other faculty than our own recognition of them. Like life, they will only be known on their own terms, whereas most prose pretends that it can be known on terms of mutual accommodation. And even prose which tries to abandon that pretence is governed by the lack of the arbitrary pattern, the ostentatiously recurrent base.

II
THE ANALYSIS OF WILLIAM

THERE are two ways of reading the *Prelude*; one is to read it as about Wordsworth, the other is to read it as about William. Wordsworth wrote a number of poems about persons with Christian names only; there are Lucy and Michael and Margaret and Leonard and Barbara and others. It seems possible to regard the *Prelude* as one of them. The point of the distinction between the two methods is not that one is superior to the other; neither is. But they define certain alternative tendencies. The reader who is more interested in Wordsworth as a personal poet and a psychological problem will tend to read it in one way; the reader who is more interested in the poetic effect of the poem the other. This will be passionately denied by all the Wordsworthians and treasured as a secret conviction by all the Williamites. It will be noticed from the last sentence that this chapter is definitely Williamite.

Let us imagine that the *Prelude* is about a person called William, to whom the things described in the poem happened and to whom, except for the irreducible minimum of natural necessity—food, sleep, &c., nothing else happened. A poem contains for itself nothing but what it does contain and nothing of what it contains exists, for poetry, outside the poem. Many poetic discoveries have been dragged out of their context and made to walk the world alone. The removal of even a stanza or line from its context tends, unless we are very careful, to

thwart it and us more than we realize. The pro-
tagonists of Shakespeare's plays, the God of *Paradise
Lost*, the William of the *Prelude*, have all suffered
in this way. But they will not endure it. The atten-
tive observer finds himself saying of them, 'Bless
thee, Bottom! bless thee! thou art translated'. Indeed they tend to be translated much as Bottom
was; over each awful countenance is imposed an
ass's head—perhaps the reader's. It may be permissible to use the *Prelude* as a whole as evidence
against Wordsworth's own fidelity to young love, or
Paradise Lost against (say) Milton's sympathy with
the Roman Church. But it is not permissible to use
Wordsworth as evidence against the William of the
Prelude or Milton as evidence against the God of
Paradise Lost. A poem with its persons and its
morality is a complete whole.

William, it seems, was a poet, and the poem has
a number of *dicta* about poetry scattered through
it; some easy, some difficult, some obvious, some
not so obvious. In many places it bears its own
testimony to the unique value of poetry. William
had a dream once in which he saw only one thing
to rival it, only one other human achievement which
was of even approximate value; that one thing was
Euclid's *Elements of Geometry*. The dream ended
before he was compelled to choose between these
two, but even in the dream poetry was thought to
be worth more than Euclid. Euclid expressed 'reason
undisturbed by space or time', but poetry expressed
passion, which itself 'is highest reason in a soul
sublime'. It is noteworthy that William did not say
that passion was like reason, or did the same work

as reason ; he said, *tout court*, that in a sublime soul passion is reason.

Sublimity nowadays is, like Wordsworth, under a cloud. It has (so we seem to feel) too often run away from its Annette of disturbing physical and mental facts and lost itself in clouds and vapours of unreal idealism. But neither Wordsworth nor William were ashamed of sublimity, as (for all we know) Wordsworth was not ashamed of Annette. He made no particular secret of her. Certainly he did not put her in the *Prelude*; I have sometimes wondered whether he omitted her because he knew she was not really important to him. Perhaps he did not cease to be a great poet (if he did) because he was too capable of detachment from Annette; perhaps he never could have been attached to Annette because he was a great poet. We have turned him lately into an example of cause and effect. But Annette, perhaps, was never important enough to be a cause of anything, nor *Vaudracour and Julia* any more autobiographical than *Paradise Lost* or *Hamlet*. It is by no means certain that great genius is so romantically attached to persons as our romantic and faithful hearts like to believe. Genius seems often to need a nodal point for its convenience, perhaps for its existence in its achievements.

> Never dare poet touch a pen to write
> Unless his ink were tempered with love's sighs.

Annette may have been a nodal point. And the reason Wordsworth said nothing more about her may have been that there was nothing more to say. How extraordinary it would be if the poets were

right in what they left out as well as in what they
put in !

At any rate William knew nothing about Annette,
and was not concerned with her. But with sublimity
both he and Wordsworth assuredly were concerned.
Wordsworth repeated the word on various occasions.
He meant by it, however, a quite definite state of
mind which he took the trouble to analyse, at least
in part. It occurs twice in *Tintern Abbey*, once in
relation to the state in which, by the power of harmony and the power of joy, 'we see into the life of
things'; the second time, as the sense aroused by
the spirit that 'rolls through all things'. The second
reference is vaguer and less convincing than the first;
the something 'whose dwelling is the light of setting
suns' is not quite satisfactory, for Wordsworth's
habitual accuracy leads us to attach importance to
the 'setting suns' as opposed to suns in any other
condition. There is a localized and slightly senti-
mental emotion in it compared to the simple universality of the rest of the definition. It has a touch of
the pseudo-romantic. He may have meant that evening is a peculiarly suitable time for such visitations,
but then he goes on to refer to the 'round ocean and
the living air, and the blue sky' in general, so that
we are defeated again. A slight pseudo-romance
does occasionally crop up in Wordsworth, and is
most to be found in certain of the most popular
pieces.

But we may take the other statement and go back
with it to the *Prelude*. Sublimity is a state in which
passion is reason; in which we see into the life of
things. It is a definition not without importance

when we consider the greatest poetry, that of the
eternal present, of 'the life of things'. In Book II
(ll. 308–22), speaking of his childhood, he describes
how he stood beneath a rock listening to the coming
storm;

> listening to notes that are
> The ghostly language of the ancient earth,
> Or make their dim abode in distant winds.
> Thence did I drink the visionary power;
> And deem not profitless those fleeting moods
> Of shadowy exultation; not for this,
> That they are kindred to our purer mind
> And intellectual life; but that the soul,
> Remembering how she felt, but what she felt
> Remembering not, retains an obscure sense
> Of possible sublimity, whereto
> With growing faculties she doth aspire,
> With faculties still growing, feeling still
> That whatsoever point they gain, they yet
> Have something to pursue.

There are three things to be remarked here,
because they were all repeated later on: (i) Visionary
power is aroused by the distant winds; (ii) this, and
such moods, are kindred to pure mind and intellectual life; (iii) they enable the soul to retain a sense
of possible sublimity—possible, and not more than
possible, because she remembers *how* but not *what*
she felt; poetry cannot yet define the *what*. She feels
that she can see into the life of things, but she does
not. Passion is reason, but she does not yet see the
rational harmony. The references were repeated
when at the end of Book V William's view of poetry
was described. A 'great Nature' exists in poetry.

Visionary power
Attends the motions of the viewless winds,
Embodied in the mystery of words :
There, darkness makes abode, and all the host
Of shadowy things work endless changes,—there,
As in a mansion like their proper home,
Even forms and substances are circumfused
By that transparent veil with light divine,
And, through the turnings intricate of verse,
Present themselves as objects recognized,
In flashes, and with glory not their own.

Visionary power again attends on the viewless
winds which belong to that Nature, but here it is
embodied in words. And there—in those words—
are recognized forms and substances; the soul knows
not merely *how* but *what* she felt. She knows power
and joy, light and glory ; which is, one may admit,
near enough to the sublimity she earlier foresaw.
And she now recognizes the forms and substances.
It seems probable that this recognition of forms and
substances, with their relations, are what William
meant by 'reason'. They are not, certainly, Euclid's
Elements; they are something more human. But
the Arab was saving the *Elements* because it was the
symbol of pure reason, and long afterwards, in the
last book, Wordsworth told us what William held
Imagination to be—

Absolute power
And clearest insight, amplitude of mind,
And Reason in her most exalted mood.

Exalted Reason then is a part of the Imagination,
of (it will be remembered) 'the Power so-called

Through sad incompetence of human speech'. It is one with the passion of sublimity. It is the intellectual life to which the distant winds of the storm are kindred, and it enables the soul to recognize forms and substances in poetry, 'with glory not their own', because of the transparent veil of the divine light of words which circumfuses them. But that is their proper home ; they exist there more truly than elsewhere. They are more themselves in poetry than in ordinary life. Reason is related to Power, for Power is its life, though, for the purpose of the poem, it is distinguished from Power. And as Euclid's *Elements* holds 'acquaintance with the stars' and presents the purest bond of Reason, so in more exalted moods Reason is the faculty by which Power discerns the life of things. But it discerns those principles not as a mere plan but as poetry.

In a long passage at the beginning of Book XIV Wordsworth described how William, with two companions, went to the top of Snowdon. He paused at an inn first; 'then, cheered by short refreshment, sallied forth'. The cause of some of Wordsworth's flatness is occasionally misunderstood ; it is that he did not like to leave anything out. We are content to live on the top of Snowdon ; we should like to build our tabernacles there. But Wordsworth, like Christ, will not have it ; he will have the bottom of the mountain as well as the top. So Milton with the Archangel's digestion ; so Shakespeare with the Countryman of Cleopatra. Those moments, indeed, are precisely the countrymen of Cleopatra ; and Cleopatra would be a poorer Egypt without them. In Shakespeare they are usually Egyptian enough for us to recognize their kinship to the Queen ; in Wordsworth they are often less Egyptian than mere country. But even the 'short refreshment' is there to take us to the top of Snowdon in every sense of the words.

At the top, however, William saw something which necessitates for us a temporary tabernacle. He saw the moon and the mists, the hills heaved up over the mists, the mists stretching away into the Atlantic, the greater stars, and the sky, and (more awful) again the moon; he heard a noise of waters, sounding as with a single voice, and seeming to be felt by the starry heavens themselves. So he went away and thought it over, recollecting his emotion in tranquillity. William's emotions needed to be recollected in tranquillity ; they were too strong to be understood at the moment. Less violent passions, in more equable minds, do not need the interval of recovery. But William recollected and reflected. And it seemed to him that all the vision was an emblem of interior power. It showed forth something actual in the nature of man: a mind that fed upon infinity—'our being's heart and home'—brooding over the abyss, intent to hear all the voices as one voice issuing into the silence and the light. This mind recognized, by means of its activity, transcendent power, and put forth power. It exercised its own domination upon the face of outward things. It and things interchange supremacy, sending abroad 'kindred mutations'. In fact, it takes things and makes poetry of them.[1] Wordsworth certainly and

[1] He even showed us how it was done. In Book XII in the passage which begins (l. 208) 'There are in our existence spots of

rightly did not limit this 'glorious faculty' to poets, he was speaking of all great minds. But certainly great poets belong to this kind of nature, for it is they also who live 'in a world of life' and not 'a universe of death'. The vision from Snowdon was that of a great poet's mind—'what in itself it is and would become'. For the desire of all poets is to be great poets, however very often their intelligence beholds the refusal of their desire; just as the desire of all morality must be for sanctity, however far off it seems to labour.

The poets, then, create an existence like the external world, 'the whole compass of the universe'. This existence—it is a shame to paraphrase a passage from which in paraphrase the power departs—is sometimes created by them and sometimes presented to them; perhaps it is not too bold to see in this the two methods by which the beginnings of a poem may be suggested—either arising from the poet's own intellectual labour or suddenly thrust on his mind by the process of things. Either way the poet is arrested by a sense of harmony; we need not underrate that word because it has so often been made so cheap. Concord of some kind, it would seem, there must be in a poem, however difficult, or it would not be a poem; it would not have a separate existence at all. Harmony does not mean the most popular tunes; it may be as difficult as we please. But wherever two things are brought into verbal

time' he described how William saw the thrilling vision of the moor, the naked pool, the beacon, and the girl carrying a pitcher and leaning against the wind. Every such moment is like a poem; the vision from Snowdon is like a great poem.

concord there must be some kind of harmony. Drama, for example, may involve clash and opposition. But without some kind of underlying harmony, it would not be drama. It would be a number of detached and unrelated elements. The beginnings of poetry (William understood) might come from anything, momentary or everlasting; the smallest suggestion is enough. Unenthralled by the world of sense, the poets are yet quickened by it. They are Powers; they exist in a world of life; and they exemplify in the highest degree that faculty which we all possess of understanding outward things in the domination of our own spirits. It is a 'glorious' faculty; let us risk one more collocation and remember that it was glory in which 'forms and substances' were recognized. William is but realizing more fully what he knew before; he is only thinking again of the 'Nature' that exists in the works of mighty poets. But here he is exemplifying his own maxim; here his genius remembers what she felt and how she felt, and his passion is itself highest Reason in his soul sublime.

Certainly there is a fact which we must remember, though he himself, merely because he was exemplifying his own maxims, omitted it; and perhaps also because of his own slight tendency to introduce religious authority into the poetic. Proclaiming in that great verse the nature of genius, he declared also that it must raise all affections 'from earth to heaven, from human to divine'; and a little later on, speaking of the progress of Imagination, he asserted that we draw from it sustaining thoughts 'Of human Being, Eternity, and God'. This particular conclusion was part of the domination over external things which William himself was taught to exercise; but it is not an inevitable part of the domination for all poets. One may remark that William did not actually see more in the mature movement of Imagination than 'the works of man and face of human life', but he did draw lessons from them and it. Other poets may not draw the same lessons; other poets exercise their domination and not his. He was dominating, even while he was describing domination. He was sending abroad mutations kindred to the universe but from his 'native self', and other poets must send them from their 'native selves'. The high description of the act is not diminished because the moral in Hardy is different from the moral in Milton. Actually, of course, we cannot truthfully compare them; for to do so we have to compare a 'form' with a 'form' and to withdraw those forms from their glory in order to do so. But it is the glory that is the only important element in the whole discussion, for the glory is the poetry, and without it the forms remain unpoetic, and therefore for the present purpose negligible.

The word 'exalted' which William in this passage thought definitive of poetic Reason recurs again at the end of the *Prelude*. It is worth noting because it there refers to a substantive which William did not so frequently name in the poem as he did Power; it qualifies Beauty—the mind of man is exalted in beauty 'above this frame of things'. William—and Samuel Taylor—are to be Prophets of Nature to men; they are to be so because they are poets (he

has, but a page or so before, been recalling their
various poems by name), and therefore the Nature
must be both that of the principles of the earth and
that which exists in the work of the poets. In an
earlier passage (vii. 759–61) he had spoken of the
Spirit of Nature, which

> aids the thoughts,
> However multitudinous, to move
> With order and relation.

It is 'the soul of Beauty and enduring Life', and
it exalted London ; it

> diffused,
> Through meagre lines and colours, and the press
> Of self-destroying, transitory things,
> Composure, and ennobling Harmony.

He did not name Beauty as an element in Imagination ; but he habitually spoke of the joy which
Beauty creates in the mind. He attended there
rather to the state of the mind creating than the
thing created. But since it is that mind which sends
vibrations abroad and since it is exalted in beauty,
we may believe that the vibrations themselves, in
bestowing composure and harmony, bestow beauty
also. William, though he realized it, did not stress
it ; he left that to other—generally lesser—poets.

The Prelude then asserts that exalted Reason is a
part of the Imagination; by Reason it means either
(i) an abstract pattern, such as Euclid or Archi-
medes produced, geometry or mathematics, the self-
consistent, unemotional world of logical creation,
or (ii) that world exalted in passion to sublimity.
And by (ii) he meant the operation of a great mind

on the forms and substances of the universe, compos-
ing and harmonizing them into a new nature within
itself. In its effective state such a mind recognizes
and unites both its own experiencing faculties and
the things it experiences. Reason without passion
and yet applied to the world is a deadly thing (the
poem earlier describes William's effort to use it so).
But when it is passion it sees into the life of things.
It beholds them, as from Snowdon; it hears ascend-
ing a single voice, which, in his own image of his
own experience, he beheld himself feeling.

There is, certainly—for good or evil—a good deal
of 'sublimity' about all this. But if it is all true, how
have the poets done it ? Power we may accept. But
in what sense has the exalted Reason been possessed
by them ? And what have they done about Beauty?

III

'WHAT IS BEAUTY?'

THERE is in *Tamburlaine* a speech of some importance to a discussion of Beauty. The theme and
figure of Tamburlaine himself are touched, after the
grand Renascence habit, with a sense of the metaphysical greatness of action. His victories are a
torrent of blood and fire, so much so that the mind
of most goodwill tends to weary before the end.
But the interest is maintained, not merely by the
magniloquence and delicacy of Marlowe's verse and
by that capacity which he has in common with all
great poets, of blasting his most monotonous verbal
habits with a phrase of catholic importance, but also
by the continual touch of philosophical greatness
in Tamburlaine himself. He is fatally destined to
conquer the world, and his nature is itself a conquest
of others. He speaks of himself, and others speak
of him, as if he possessed a greater share of divine
elemental power than the rest of the world, as if he
were, in a different mode, one of the Powers in
whom William believed. He is a man ordained 'to
further every action to the best'. He kills his son
for his cowardice, but that cowardice is a sign of
the difference between such 'scum and tartar of the
elements' and his own body in which an incorporeal
spirit of Jove's own mould moves. He also is 'truly
from the Deity', just as William saw. The verses
in which he proposes to ride through Samarkand
as emperor look forward to his spirit's ascension
through the milk-white way to meet Jove, his great

exemplar. His captains implore the gods to preserve
his life by invocation of their sanctity:

> If you retain desert of holiness,
> As your supreme estates instruct our thought;

the physicians warn him of danger because a substance more divine and pure than the elements is
almost extinguished in him. They would not perhaps
have held him different from other men in this, but
their science here confirms the general view of Tamburlaine. He and Theridamas admire each other so
inevitably that when Theridamas deserts the Persian
King he only seems to show the magnanimity 'that
nobly must admit necessity'. The emperor's personal appearance is described in similar terms: his
face has a pallor 'wrought in him with passion'.
It is the misfortune of the world's lowness that he
appears in it as a conqueror; he was meant for
deeds of 'bounty and nobility'. His thoughts are
pure and fiery, and among those thoughts are his
description of the nature of the souls of men and
his meditations on Zenocrate.

His own soul can begin to comprehend the
wondrous architecture of the world. It is such a
faculty of comprehension which leads him to question himself upon the nature of his love. But the
speech in which he does so is almost a document of
aesthetics, for it is a statement of man's apprehension of beauty. Zenocrate herself is in distress at
the battle between her husband's and her father's
armies, and Tamburlaine is troubled by her tears.
Her sorrows shake him more than his armies
Damascus, her father's city. So far the speech is no

more than a magniloquent description of a conventional state. But from now on the inquiry becomes more passionately abstract. Beauty (of course) sits in Zenocrate's face, 'and comments volumes with her ivory pen'; she was to do as much and more in *Love's Labour's Lost* when Berowne was eloquent on women's eyes. But where Berowne was to be mostly aware of the increased power which beauty, and love arising from beauty, give to all capacities, Tamburlaine is aware of something not only different but opposite. The beauty of Zenocrate arouses in him something which no hostile army had ever stirred, a sense of defeat, a 'conceit of foil'. It is a physical sensation of extreme force; kings have not troubled him 'so much, by much'. It might be held from what we have been told and seen earlier, that no king had ever troubled him with any conceit of foil at all, but Marlowe was not then bothering about consistency. The 'so much, by much' does its work, and we are made aware of the defeat which Beauty causes in his and our spirits, and even of the distress by which that sensation of overthrow is accompanied. Man beholds Beauty, endures this conceit of foil, and inevitably and immediately demands to know its nature. 'What is beauty? saith my sufferings then.' Tamburlaine, soaring into the poetic heaven of Marlowe's mind, answers himself by a sudden consideration not only of beauty but of poetry. For (he says) man's mind is most expressed in poetry; there, as in a mirror, we behold the highest reaches of a human wit. Forms and substances, in fact, exist there in the most sublime state. William and Christopher would have adored each other.

We understand in poetry the greatest extent of
our knowledge; that knowledge which can comprehend the world's architecture, as he had told us
before. But here is something it cannot comprehend. Our souls that can measure the wandering
planets' courses and climb after knowledge infinite,
and poetry which mirrors all our knowledge, are
here defeated. There is something in Beauty which
poetry cannot express, and which the poets—and
Tamburlaine and we—know they cannot express.
The quintessence of all poetry in one poem, could it
be so collected, would still leave something untold.
This is the answer given to the question his suffering is compelled to ask; this, then, is why he suffers.
Beauty inflicts on man everlasting defeat because
in the end man cannot discover and express it in
poetry, therefore not at all. The mind of man discovers that it is not equivalent to the nature of
Beauty.

At this point Tamburlaine begins to recall himself to his own nature, and, as it were, away from
Marlowe's. But the identification of himself with
Marlowe is not entirely lost; the invocation of the
poetry has been too strong. He reminds himself of
his sex, his 'discipline of arms and chivalry'; in spite
of that conceit of foil he forbids himself to harbour
'thoughts effeminate and faint'. Nevertheless, Beauty,
'with whose instinct the soul of man is touched',
affects warriors; all who are rapt with love of fame,
valour, and victory must of necessity endure also this
experience of Beauty. They must have it 'beat on
their conceits', and the word recalls its earlier use;
their very conceits must know their conceit of foil.

This sensation of defeat and contemporaneous refusal of effeminate thoughts combine in the next
lines:

> I thus conceiving and subduing both
> That which hath stoopt the tempest of the gods
> To feel the lovely warmth of shepherds' flames,
> And march in cottages of strowed weeds—

It is still Beauty; it is Beauty which has itself
subdued a divine tumult into the comfort of huts
and domestic fires. But it is Beauty not among cot-
tages and shepherds' flames but in itself which this
Tamburlaine-Marlowe, this warrior-poet, will subdue. He will 'conceive' it; that is, among his own
conceits he will apprehend this overthrow of himself
by a wonder impossible for any virtue of words to
express, and then he will conquer it. And in that
conquest of Beauty, herself the conquering mistress
of the tempest of the gods, it will be seen

> That virtue solely is the sum of glory
> And fashions men with true nobility.

He then departs to battle.

He has been speaking as a warrior. But the lines
about poetry are a part of the whole speech, and
were not written only for the anthologies in which
they have, very naturally, so often appeared. It was
into words that no virtue could digest the full wonder of Beauty, and the virtue which, sixteen lines
later, concludes the speech is not certainly an entirely different power. The sum of glory for the
Tamburlaine of the play may have been the virtue
of conquest and royalty. It was his business to win

battles. But it was Marlowe's to write poems. The
sum of glory for that 'pure elemental wit' (as
Thomas Thorpe called him) who wrote the play
was the conceiving and subduing beauty in words.
The nobility of the poets is their refusal to harbour
thoughts effeminate and faint; it is, in fact, their
courage to write poetry. Courage is a virtue not
generally attributed to poets, yet it is a necessity
of their nature. It requires courage to dare the
abyss from which Wordsworth beheld the power of
Imagination arise, to contemplate it till the forms
and substances are exactly discovered. In that abyss
they are to conceive and subdue 'that which hath
stoopt the tempest of the gods', to control their
greatest idea of the greatest power. Marlowe declared that it could not be done, but, on the other
hand, he declared also that it was the poet's virtue
to do it.

The speech then, to some extent, illumines the
poets' business. They are to 'conceive' the complete
power of Beauty, with all its continual inexpressible
wonders, and to express it. But they do not do it in
quite the straightforward way in which Tamburlaine
proceeded to defeat the army of the Sultan, or Marlowe described that defeat. The direct attack on
Beauty has a tendency to lead to rhetoric and even to
rant. In order to achieve its end, English poetry
has had to go a long way round; in order to digest all
Beauty's graces into words it has had to digest some
remarkably strange food. It has had to discover
defeats more terrible than the exquisitely painful and
joyous overthrow of man's spirit by Beauty, and
sufferings less immediately recompensed than those.

In such defeat and suffering the virtue and nobility of the poets has had every opportunity to make itself known.

But to explore the process by which poetry exalted Reason and conceived the perfection of Beauty, we may begin with a poem which limited itself severely in its devotion to both, with Pope's *Essay on Man*.

IV
'REASONING BUT TO ERR'
THE *ESSAY ON MAN*

IF the distinction between prose and poetry which
is contained in the first of these essays is at all
valid, it will be clear why philosophical argument
in verse is likely to be unsatisfactory. It will not
only fail to please because our romanticism desires
from poetry always the high lights and the intense
moment, the vision from Snowdon or the Nightingale in song, but because our consideration of the
argument is distracted by a too vivid awareness of
the pattern, and therefore of that individualizing,
that limitation of the argument which, though it is
turned into an added pleasure, persuades us that we
are not persuaded. 'I am telling you,' says that
continually recurrent base; 'I am not persuading
you. I am being myself; I am not really bothering
about you. I am that I am.' The intuitive rightness of the poetic rhythms are not always united
with the discursive rightness of the argument; as
so often in our own lives, one generally has to run
after the other. Either the rhythms are abandoned
for the argument, and the metre becomes lacka-
daisical, or the argument for the rhythms, and the
discursive reason is left behind, pointing out the
fallacies.

It is a great pity therefore that my Lord Bolingbroke did not supply Mr. Pope with better arguments, because if he had we might have had a
really good example in the *Essay on Man* of the best

that could be done in this kind. As it is, the best poet of the Age of Reason is rather unsuccessful with his reasoning. Pope has been called witty rather than poetic; he has been refused the title of poet. But his arrows are Apollonian, even if they are barbed with wit, and even if Apollo was never so near acting on Nihilistic principles in his own kingdom. It is a little unfortunate that we have got so into the habit of talking of Pope's couplets; our attention has induced in us a belief that his genius is in his couplets, in their balance and in their conclusion, and that their intellect closes with their rhyme. And no doubt this is a very important part of his method. But we need not make it more important than it is, and in fact we have a little neglected both his single lines and his paragraphs. The single line in Pope often goes farther than the couplet; his flights return upon themselves in the second line, and in the contact achieved we forget the course traversed. And similarly we forget the paragraph.

Yet to forget the line and the paragraph is to forget Pope's distances and his architecture, it is to confine him to a two-story house, whereas the gardens of his single lines are larger, though they lead back to the house, and there are towers overlooking a wider prospect. It is certainly rather a town prospect; his poetry is as metropolitan as the tall column he denounced (and the denunciation sometimes fits him too). But whatever our grandfathers may have thought, we nowadays are free from the illusion that the country is more poetic than the town, or peers less poignant than peasants.

Pope preferred peers as Wordsworth preferred peasants. On the whole, judging by the plays, Shakespeare preferred peers too. At any rate, what Pope surveyed he surveyed from the paragraph as well as the couplet. Certain of those gathered and accumulated energies are remembered—the attack on Addison, the close of the *Dunciad*, the 'Know then thyself' passage from the *Essay on Man*. But he is more habitually accumulative than those few passages suggest. The opening of the *Essay on Criticism* has a similar growth in force ; so has that later paragraph of which the first line is so widely and so wrongly known.

> A little Learning is a dangerous thing ;
> Drink deep, or taste not the Pierian spring :
> There shallow draughts intoxicate the brain,
> And drinking largely sobers us again.
> Fired at first sight with what the Muse imparts,
> In fearless youth we tempt the heights of Arts,
> While from the bounded level of our mind
> Short views we take nor see the lengths behind ;
> But more advanced, behold with strange surprise
> New, distant scenes of endless science rise !
> So pleased at first the towering Alps we try,
> Mount o'er the vales, and seem to tread the sky,
> Th' eternal snows appear already past,
> And the first clouds and mountains seem the last :
> But those attained, we tremble to survey
> The growing labours of the lengthened way,
> Th' increasing prospect tires our wandering eyes,
> Hills peep o'er hills, and Alps on Alps arise !

It is, if the reader will accept the habit of the verse, an exact statement not merely of the effect of learning but of verse. Did not the 'shallow draughts' of poetry first intoxicate us? and are we not sobered by the larger drinking of Milton or Wordsworth? 'The eternal snows appear already past' when we have tried the Alps of Blake's or Shelley's lyrics. But many a reader has trembled to survey *Paradise Lost* or the *Prelude*, and much of Shakespeare's popularity is due to the fact that each play is considerably shorter than either of those other ranges. 'Our wandering eyes'—precisely. The thrill of poetry takes us all at first, and then we think we have attained everything. It is a dangerous illusion; drink deep or taste not.

Again, the mistrust with which the poetry of the eighteenth century was regarded robbed us of our proper understanding of what sometimes they were doing. Swift has suffered from it perhaps more even than Pope. 'Cousin Jonathan, you will never be a poet'; we have all believed Dryden. But in fact Swift was a poet, sometimes horrible, sometimes exquisite. The fact that his verse is sometimes disgusting ought not to conceal the fact that our disgust is partly the achievement of the verse. The emotional Manichaeanism which in Swift conflicted with an intellectual orthodoxy provoked him to be horrid. But something other than that provoked him to be serious. There is in much of his verse a medieval dance of death and hate carried into the Augustan boudoirs. But the hate disappears and the death, though it remains, moves to a grave human measure.

> Poor Pope will grieve a month, and Gay
> A week, and Arbuthnot a day,

St. John himself will scarce forbear
To bite his pen and drop a tear.

There is not much romantic agony about that, certainly, so we have hastily called it ironic. But it is not ironic, nor scornful, nor anything but merely actuality circumfused by poetry. It is one of those passages, scattered through English verse, which remind us of the later Shakespeare, though it has less power and deals with less intense things, with outer habits rather than inner life. But here also is a substance of human life, a fact of existence, recognized for a flash and with glory not its own. It is not as full of splendour as almost any stanza of *Adonais*, but it is much more of the substance of ordinary existence. It is accurate and tender at once; a mortal light breaks from it; why must we ask for other poetic beauty, neglecting its own? 'Poor Pope will grieve a month'; let us be quite honest and ask for which of our friends we should come anywhere near anything that could be called grieving for anything like a month. And which of them for us?

'Follow nature', wrote Pope:

Art from that fund each just supply provides,
Works without show, and without pomp presides.

It is hardly a sufficient description of the great poets when they let themselves go. But it is much more like a statement of them at their greatest moments. 'Works without show'—and Miranda? and the conclusions of the *Paradises*? and the noblest lines of the *Prelude*? Pope did not always follow his own maxim; he mixed his personal tastes with nature too much. But sometimes it is Nature and not his personal tastes that he is following. He has been labelled ironical, and so he must always be ironical. But hear the dying Narcissa:

> One would not, sure, be frightful when one's dead:
> So—Betty, give this cheek a little red.

Is that pure satire? and not satire grown a little tender? Life is satirical enough, but never merely satirical, and Pope recognized all the elements and exquisitely carried them over. It is Nature in his work which creates half his power; it is his own mind which creates the other half. And sometimes those two powers were at loggerheads.

'The ruling passion conquers reason still.' Reason in Pope is generally intellectual argument; it is sometimes common sense. We are to avoid the extreme, even in appreciation. 'Fools admire, but men of sense approve.' The irony of the Muse 'getting back' on Pope has made it very difficult to approve, though we may in the full sense admire him. Yet our admiration is usually complete at first whenever we do admire. His maxims generally may be proved by more and more examples, but they do not become in themselves more wonderful or more profound. 'Some made coxcombs nature meant but fools' is a line of which our own lives show us in ourselves and others many instances. But there will never be anything more to discover in the line. It is a compressed felicity of the intelligence.

Yet sometimes something more than the compression of the discursive reason appears; some intuition of poetry,

Taught, half by reason, half by mere decay,
To welcome death, and calmly pass away.

Strictly, Pope might have found that couplet out by reasoning; it is clear to men of sense. But either the word 'decay' or the arbitrary pattern and energy of the couplet impose it on us more strongly than the lines we recognize chiefly with our applauding minds. 'Nature' has come in, the nature that exists in the works of the mighty poets. There is an echo of the sounds that are 'the ghostly language of the antique earth'. It is apt to come in—and sometimes when Pope, for all we can see, did not want it as well as when he apparently did.

The *Essay on Man* is the great example of this. Pope, it is well known, was a Roman Catholic. Only the more devout members of his Church would recognize it from his verse.[1] But certainly the moral of the *Essay on Man* was the moral of Dante and the Lady Julian of Norwich. 'Whatever is, is right.' 'What then can be amiss?' No believer in God has yet been able to answer that last question by reasoning against it. Pope's reasoning is hampered by (i) his refusal to let reason go too far, (ii) the poem's uncertainty about its use of the word God, (iii) and most important—the sudden appearance at odd moments of a poetic energy, of a different kind of 'Nature'.

Over the first limitation we need not delay. It is presumably responsible for the deplorable lapses in

---

[1] I should not myself have thought any one would have recognized it. But Mr. Shane Leslie, in his *Anthology of Catholic Poets*, has included six extracts, including the *Elegy on an Unfortunate Lady* and I accept Pope's co-religionist's decision.

the argument. We are to reason, that is—to argue, up to a certain point, but then to stop. 'In pride, in reasoning pride, our error lies.' Pope's error certainly did not lie in reasoning pride. It more probably lay in the second limitation; in his incapacity to make up his mind whether he was or was not going to 'scan' God. 'The proper study of mankind is man.' Very well; but why then lead us to such conclusions as that

> the Universal Cause
> Acts not by partial but by general laws?

Consequently, He cannot stop a landslide when 'blameless Bethel' happens to be passing. He is not prone to reverse his laws for his favourites. But since, when God determined to allow landslides, He must have foreseen Mr. Bethel's proximity, it would seem that His responsibility remains. 'Hard cases' must be taken account of in the economy of Omniscience; Pope would turn it into something like the working of English law, which (as we know) cannot reckon with them. The argument is not even puerile; it is babyish. Much better leave God alone.

When, however, Pope did, when he forgot his argument for one or a couple or a dozen lines, something altogether different happened. Curiously enough, the first example happens at the very beginning of the poem.

> Awake, my St. John! leave all meaner things
> To low ambition and the pride of kings.
> Let us (since life can little more supply
> Than just to look about us and to die)
> Expatiate free o'er all this scene of man—

The parenthesis has very nearly destroyed the

poem; it has certainly shaken it very seriously. What! when life is like that, when the sudden vision of things sees them so, are we to be amused with expatiation? 'To look about us and to die', 'expatiate free', the directness of the first seven words cancels the intention of the other two. Death has already abolished this scene of man, the 'mighty maze, but not without a plan'; we have glanced at its complexities and are already vanishing. The real poetic energy of Pope freed his intellect from its duty to argue; his reason in her own most exalted mood swept away his reasoning explanations. The passion that is reason awoke and the reason that is not passion was abolished.

However, he went on with the poem. But Nihilism kept breaking in. We must, he said piously, be careful not to argue too far. Still, so far as we do humbly argue, we may accept our conclusion that whatever is—Mr. Bethel crushed by the landslide or what not—'is right'. May we? What lies near, when we take to our proper study of man?

He hangs between; in doubt to act, or rest;
In doubt to deem himself a God, or beast;
In doubt his mind or body to prefer;
Born but to die, and reas'ning but to err;
Alike in ignorance, his reason such,
Whether he thinks too little or too much:
Chaos of thought and passion, all confus'd;
Still by himself abus'd or disabus'd;
Created half to rise, and half to fall;
Great lord of all things, yet a prey to all;
Sole judge of truth, in endless error hurl'd:
The glory, jest, and riddle of the world!

Pope took that from Pascal, no doubt; but there is still less doubt that he knew what he wanted when he took it.

One other example (there are more) will serve. He was, as has been said, a Catholic. And towards the end of the same book which opens with that last great mockery, he speaks of the properties of his creed.

> Behold the child, by nature's kindly law,
> Pleas'd with a rattle, tickled with a straw:
> Some livelier play-thing gives his youth delight,
> A little louder, but as empty quite:
> Scarfs, garters, gold, amuse his riper stage,
> And beads and prayer-books are the toys of age:
> Pleased with this bauble still, as that before;
> Till tired he sleeps, and life's poor play is o'er.

'Pleased with this bauble still, as that before.' It is almost the comment of the whole poem.

> Opinion gilds with varying rays
> Those painted clouds that beautify our days;
> Each want of happiness by hope supplied—

Hope comes out of the poem very badly. It is, as it were, the word about which Pope's conflict goes on. Is hope really a divine comfort or a silly deception?

> Hope springs eternal in the human breast:
> Man never is, but always to be blest.

> See some fit passion every age supply,
> Hope travels through, nor quits us when we die.

Pope never quite made up his mind whether he said 'hope' as a prayer or a sneer. But if he had he would have been a less fascinating poet; if, to use our

modern slang, he could ever have resolved his own
conflict. He certainly did not resolve it in his poem
on life in general. There the passion that is reason
and the reasoning that is not passionate contend,
and the reasoning, so often overthrown, pulls itself
together again and toils on to its hopeless assertion
of hope. It even sinks at times to such lines as

> Why has not man a microscopic eye?
> For this plain reason, man is not a fly;

or finds itself reduced to

> All this dread order breaks for whom? for thee?
> Vile worm!—oh madness! pride! impiety!

And whenever it produced 'my St. John's' lucid
perception of desirable behaviour or desirable belief,
the more intense perception in Pope's own spirit over-
came it. He confronted and analysed his moments
of Nihilism when they occurred because he was a
poet; but because he was not a great poet he did
not drag that very Nihilism itself into the open. He
was content to leave the thrilling line 'born but to
die and reasoning but to err' in close propinquity
with the many lines which use reasoning. He tried
sometimes to make peace by warning us not to carry
our reasoning pride too far. But not to carry reasoning pride too far is one thing, and to know that error
is the end of all reasoning is quite another. So he declared that religion is a proper and necessary thing;
but his genius knew that 'beads and prayer-books are
the toys of age'. 'Whatever is, is right'; it is right,
then, that man should be 'the glory, jest, and riddle
of the world'. No doubt it may be, but to make both
lines credible it is necessary to examine that riddle a

little more closely and solve it more exactly than Pope chose to do. Otherwise the triumphant 'glory' of the line that proclaims it will dim the milder glory of the other line which procrastinates about it.

He composed his philosophical poem under the threat of his 'ruling passion'. But that ruling passion was itself divided. It was aware of those states of dark realism which it at times expressed; it was also aware of the danger—not so much to poetry as to life—that lay in them. It sought therefore to banish or control them. The whole astonishing effort of the eighteenth century moved in the same way; but it failed, and it failed partly because it attempted to lock its skeleton in its cupboard. A book of some interest might be written upon English literature through the ages under the title of *The Skeleton*— how the Elizabethans bragged about it and the Jacobeans intellectualized it, and the Augustans shut it up, and the earlier Romantics, in the excitement of finding it was there, let it partly out, and the curious energy of Beddoes and Hood tried to let it wholly out, and the Victorians, meeting it, chained it and refused to make an intimate of it, and since the Victorians we have not at all agreed what to do with it. For it has been received as a new discovery— which is silly; and denied as morbid and unhealthy —which is sillier; and anatomized at great length —which is interesting but transitory; and transmuted into sex problems or political problems— which is still more transitory; and even made into a guardian of rather superior intellectual society— which is the silliest and most transitory of all. Every age, like every poet and every man, has the skeleton

that it deserves; the life of the skeleton is its own
doubled life, and marriage with the skeleton is perhaps after all the wisest intercourse with it—meaning by that all that marriage involves of intimacy
and of strangeness, of friendship and hostility, of
freedom and captivity, and something like a new
life. But of the child of that marriage there are
different opinions; for some say it is the new life
in God, and some call it illusion and bitterness,
and some hold that it is the power of Shakespeare's
latest plays, and some that it is the philosophy of
Hardy's verse. So perhaps they all are right and
the child of the skeleton is a being we shall never
understand till we have become skeletons ourselves,
if then. But that it has always been the closest
neighbour of mankind, and a continual intimate of
the genius of the poets there is no doubt at all. And
the hand of Pope lay on it though only to push it
back into the cell where the Augustans, after the
experience of it which the last couple of centuries
of their fathers had endured, desired to keep it.
However, they failed.

Yet something of the energy of that remarkable
Anatomy (as the Elizabethans would have called it)
passed into them none the less, perhaps because
their refusal of it was that of judgement and not of
fear. It entered into Pope's personal quarrels; it
walked in Swift's horrible indecencies. It gave them
epigrams of malice—'Poxed by her love or slandered
by her hate'; or that other couplet which so destruc-
tively outgoes the more famous lines that follow it:

How did they fume, and stamp, and roar, and chafe !
And swear not Addison himself is safe !

For in matters of his personal quarrels or his study of letters Pope had no need to deny his perceptions for the sake of his philosophy; that is, to divide his poetic intellect against itself. He may have been wrong, but he was not doubtful. There he deliberately invoked the triumph of the Anatomy, of all that he hated—the close of the *Dunciad* is its expression—in order that he might denounce it. At the point where sense and dullness meet he dared the advance of dullness. The geometry of his poetic rules and the power of his poetic genius there became one; on his own dromedary he fled with them to save them from the light that shone on the waters of the deep—the romantic deep yet unrealized—gathering upon him. The Arab's stone and shell were lifted in a single hand, and sang the ruling passion of his heart for what he believed was the nature of poetry.

V
THE EVASION OF IDENTITY
(i) SPENSER

IN a cave of Faeryland, a low cave under a great cliff, surrounded by the stocks and stubs of trees where nothing had hung but dead men whose bodies were strewn over the grass and about the cliff, while the owl shrieked from the height and only the wails of wandering ghosts answered him—in so romantic, likely, and unlikely a place St. George encountered Despair. Despair himself was equally adequate to the enforced occasion ; he was attired suitably, and was sitting by a still-bleeding corpse, 'musing full sadly in his sullen mind'. Nothing could be more exquisitely told ; the owl itself, in that symbolical state, has rarely been so melodious. One has but to remember the owl that appears after Lady Macbeth's dreadful exclamation :

Peace !
It was the owl that shrieked, that fatal bellman,

to recognize at once the difference between Faeryland and Inverness.

But that exquisite transmutation is only a part of the change. For any one who attends to the dialogue between St. George and the damnèd wight with whom he speaks will soon notice that another alteration, and a much more surprising one, is in progress. Despair is unexpectedly turning into Hope, and a very persuasive Hope at that. A few lines from his speeches will show it.

He there does now enjoy eternal rest
And happy ease, which thou dost want and crave.
Sleep after toil, port after stormy seas,
Ease after war, death after life does greatly please.
Death is the end of woes; die soon, O faery's son.

The unsurpassable sweetness of that line is almost enough to persuade any one to ensue death. But it is death as the end of woes that is promised, and it is the hope, even the promise, of that which so moves the Red Cross Knight. It is true that Despair also works on St. George's religious fear of his sins and the hell they have deserved, urging him to run no risk of adding to their number and his suffering. But even there it is combined hope and despair which is used. There is no hope in this life; but there is hope that death may end the sin and lessen the pain—'die soon, O faery's son'.

It was, when one comes to think of it, inevitable that this should happen. Spenser was a master of many kinds of music, but not of the intense and intellectual music that is needed to express real Despair; we have to find that in another poet—with a prose-writer between to link them, as it were. For though Despair may for most of us be a state where we have no hope but of death, yet still that hope of death is a hope, and the despair is therefore not complete. 'Wanhope' was the old Saxon word, and we might well revive it in order to express that state, keeping the word 'Despair' for the utter hopelessness in which there is no promise at all. That is not in Spenser, but in Milton; and between them is Bunyan. In the castle of Giant Despair Christian and Hopeful also are tempted to kill themselves; but the Giant does not lure them with such exquisite phrases. 'Death is the end of woes' makes death itself beautiful; at a distance it hints towards the richer Death of the *Ode to a Nightingale*. There it is rich to die, because that death is the loss of life in immortal life; here Death is (as Keats said) 'easeful', but no more; what Keats went on to imagine, Spenser let alone. Spenser, nevertheless, was precisely calling Death soft names in many a musèd rhyme. But Bunyan lacked both musèd rhyme and soft names. In the *Pilgrim's Progress* Death is felt and known as the cessation of an unbearable anguish; but it is the anguish we know and not the cessation. In Spenser we enjoy the cessation; in Bunyan we only know that the anguish need not continue. But in Milton we do not even know that, for the anguish must continue, and therefore we are enlarged to a knowledge of complete despair. The most that can there be hoped is to be at the worst—

> To whom the Tempter, inly racked, replied . .
> I would be at the worst; worst is my port,
> My harbour and my ultimate repose.

Paradise Regained it is which contains that awful definition of the other side of hope; but, terrible as the three lines are, the last two enlarging and defining the 'inly racked' of the first, it is still to *Paradise Lost* we must go for the full expression. There, in the Niphates speech, we have it; there is complete despair, without any hope at all of cessation or even change except for worse.

> In the lowest deep a lower deep,
> Still gaping to devour me, opens wide,
> To which the hell I suffer seems a heaven.

And afterwards comes the complete break, the identity of Despair expressed; beyond Spenser and beyond Bunyan comes the sound of a separation deeper than they knew : 'Farewell, Hope.'

Compare with those words Spenser's 'Death is the end of woes', and we have one reason why Milton is a greater poet than Spenser : forms and substances are in him more fully and finally imagined.

We are sometimes told that we need not bother about Spenser's allegory; that he did not bother about it himself. The second assurance is to some extent true; but he thought he did—poor darling! He wrote a long explanation of it. And it seems a little ungrateful to him and a little negligent of poetry if we are so ready to omit an element which Spenser deliberately inserted. Only we ought to be clear what we are asked to enjoy, and perhaps the word used above may help : there is not, in Spenser, the *identity* of Despair. All his caves and cliffs and owls and corpses, thorn-stitched garments and hollow eyne, will not make that poetic identity sure. It is allegory, but it is not identity. The *O.E.D.* defines allegory as a 'narrative speaking of a subject under guise of another suggestively similar'. Suggestively similar. But to be similar, even to be suggestively similar, and to be identical are two different things, and even a poet can hardly manage both at once.

One of the greatest examples of identity in all poetry is Dante's Beatrice. It seems extraordinary that learned men should have discussed whether Beatrice was Theology, and thought that their affirmative answer meant that Beatrice was not a woman. She is, of course, Theology because she is a woman;

she is a given fact which has in two categories
of experience two different names. But the fact
itself is identical everywhere. Dante may have
been merely insane when he believed this; as any
other lover may who believes that the wrists of
his lady are moral goodness, or her forehead ab-
original light, or her hands executive intelligence.
He may; or he may be entirely sane. The important
thing is that no one in that state of apprehension,
false or true, has any belief in 'suggestive similarity'.
The 'dark conceit' in his mind is a quite different
thing from the 'dark conceit' which Spenser said the
Faerie Queene was. Symbolism it may be, because
(as Coleridge told us) a symbol has its own being,
as well as being a part of some other greater being,
and representing the whole of that greater being in
its own part. But allegory it is not.

It is therefore no use asking Spenser to give
us such figures as Dante—making Beatrice one
with Theology—or Milton—making Satan one with
Despair—or Shakespeare—making Macbeth one with
murder. For identities of that kind we have to start
with figures as intensely themselves as can be man-
aged; the less themselves they are, the less identical
with facts of another category they become. But the
more themselves they are, the less 'suggestively
similar' of another kind of fact can they be. This
is the law of symbolism—that the symbol must
be utterly itself before it can properly be a symbol. But the more himself a man is the less is he
likely to be *similar* to anything, even a virtue; for
virtue and vice are to us only known by men.
But similarity was what Spenser wanted, and the

intellectual side of his poem was concerned with that similarity.

It is not primarily a poetic quality, as the philosophy of the *Essay on Man* is not primarily poetic. It is doctrinal; at least there seems to be no reason why you should concentrate on suggestive similarities between imagined human beings and abstract virtues and vices unless there is some kind of doctrine about somewhere. Doctrine, of course, may be an intense part of poetry; but in that case it must arise for us out of the poetry. But allegory tends to prevent this, because allegory is too soon aware of its own end. The conclusion of every poem ought to follow upon the poetry of its own 'reason in its most exalted mood'; so ought any doctrine it may happen to impart. But allegory tends to start in reason in her less exalted mood, and to be uneasily aware of this start all the way through.

Indeed not the least important part of the reading of poetry is the attention that must be paid to the poem's own consciousness—if so solemn a word may be permitted. Anything may be seen in a poem, but nothing unavoidable should be put in. It is, for instance, very easy to put into *Julius Caesar* our own political views about Caesar, or to inject into the *Idylls of the King* our antiquarian knowledge of the Celtic sources of the Grail legends. It is the less important poems usually, and fortunately, which suffer most from this injection; the more important are generally strong enough to refuse it. But even with them there is a danger; for example, the problem of Banquo's guilt has been put into *Macbeth*, when it seems that the poem does not wish to bother itself either way, and (contrariwise) it is very easy to want to insert into *Lycidas* our own lack of concern with the habits of parish priests. But *Lycidas*, whether we like it or not, is concerned with the habits of parish priests, and *Macbeth* is not concerned with the guilt of Banquo. Catholicism is inserted into the *Unknown Eros* and Puritanism into *Paradise Lost*; no doubt in each there are traces of those respective elements, but the traces are small when compared with the nuggets with which the prospectors return. Poems can be salted as well as mines in the interests of a company whose business is with this or that product but not with poetry—which, after all, is the actual cause of the mine.

The poets themselves are sometimes responsible. Tennyson, for example, announced that he had put a great deal of doctrine of sorts into the *Idylls of the King*. Here and there it is recognizable—in the Coming and Departure of Arthur, or in the moment when at Arthur's coronation the Lady of the Lake remembers that she is the Church. But in general the poem forgets its concern in its preoccupation with natural life and with a reverie of grief. The allegory there can hardly be said to be part of the poem at all. But in the *Faerie Queene* it is much more generally present. A poem which has Sansfoy, Sansjoy, and Sansloy in it; and the House of Holiness; and Archimago; and Mammon and Despair and Slander, and so on, can hardly be accused of forgetting that it means to contain 'suggestive similarities'. Yet those same similarities are, by common consent, remote from the finest poetry, and one cause of this at any rate is clear. It is that the persons of the poem can but convey an attributed passion. Attributed passion is a necessity of the poem. If you wish to write an allegorical poem about courage, and bring in courage as such, there are only two things to do (i) put it in, personified, under its own name, as some of the Moralities and Interludes did; in which case courage will tend to become monotonous. Or (ii) say, in effect: 'I wish to write a poem about Courage, but either because I fear this will bore you or because I derive pleasure from having complications, I shall call Courage by the name of Lord Tomtit, and describe its process to you under the guise of Lord Tomtit's adventures.' This method may be and often is very curious and delightful; it has but one difficulty, which is that in proportion as Lord Tomtit is suggestively similar to Courage he will tend to lose all capacity for being courageous. If your only hypothesis of existence for a certain character is a certain quality, it is impossible for you to give effective examples of that quality in that character, since without its quality it exists, not less nobly, but not at all. We have therefore to attribute to him the very passion he is himself presenting; we must believe him to be courageous lest he should lose the capacity for the quality in his personification of that quality. It is difficult even for Sir Guyon to be temperate and Temperance at once. Even Britomart manages to be Chastity only because of her preoccupation with a love which becomes in so many ladies the opposite of Chastity. But Britomart is exceptionally fortunate because she—and we—can look forward to her enjoyment of Chastity's, let us say, fulfilment in its

union with married love. Neither Guyon nor Cali-
dore will ever be so happily combined with indulgence or rudeness. We have therefore to attribute
to all those high ideas the passion which we feel for
them and which they are supposed to feel. But we
cannot attribute tragedy, and in fact no tragic crisis
can exist in a moral allegory, since a tragic crisis
depends on human figures. Yet all human morality
is likely at any moment to involve a tragic crisis.
The poem, therefore, seems to have forbidden itself
the most intense kind of poetry.

Spenser forbade us tragedy; he demanded of
us attributed passion. Such decisions were in the
nature of his genius, which existed precisely in the
communication of rich convolutions of magnificent
fantasy, against which sometimes a simple fantasy
would be thrown up. There is, for example, no
fighting in him. The battle between St. George
and the Dragon coils its exquisite length through
fifty-five stanzas—about five hundred lines, and
every ninth wave contains the full, solemn, and
periodical sensation of temporary conclusion and interval. That over such great spaces Spenser should
avoid monotony is the fact of his genius for the use
of words. There is in him a kind of innocent insolence; the insolence is in his luxurious rhythms
and the innocence in his bright fresh diction; his
invention of word and movement drives two ways
at once, combining their suggestive similarities.
Or, indeed, even more ways, if we take account of
the personal figures whom those fabulous figures
convey, Lord Grey of Wilton and the Earl of
Leicester, and such like historicities. For so the

complexity becomes (for him) more complex and
more enjoyable. We may not read Spenser often,
but when we do we are always entertained.

Nevertheless, it is an entertainment which abandons the Wordsworthian Reason, because Reason
is subordinated to the poetic needs of the poem.
This would be well enough if we could believe it
were also identified with those poetic needs. But
it is hardly that. The Red Cross Knight, who is
Holiness, is tempted by Despair, and that, even
though Despair is Hope, we may pass. But why
should Temperance be overthrown by Chastity at
the opening of the third Book ? To put it so is to
suggest at once the very intense poetic and even
speculative ideas which from time to time begin
to arise. But because the Reason of the poem is
imposed from without, and its poetic energy is in its
luxury rather than its rationality, the crisis is avoided.
We are not in the kind of poem which deals with
so intense a philosophical imagination. Our awakened intellects pant for the sequel ; what splendour
of vision is to follow? Alas, what does follow is
almost funny. Temperance is angry and Magnificence has to soothe him. Prince Arthur lays the
misfortune

> to the ill purveyance of his page
> That had his furniture not firmly tied.

I cannot think it really magnanimous in Magnificence to blame the wretched page, even if there
had been a page to blame, but we have not heard of
one, though indeed a page or two is neither here nor
there in Spenser. So Temperance and Chastity are
reconciled, and exchange gifts, and for a little the

mere involutions of beauty almost persuade us that high symbolism and great identity are there after all.

Spenser had a simple mind and complex tastes (unlike Bunyan, who had a complex mind and simple tastes), and his simple mind, absorbed in his tastes, became arbitrary with his dark conceit. Poetry and Reason lie down together like the lion and the lamb; but in the end the smile (to vary the metaphor) is always on the face of the tiger. In the person of Britomart the tiger and the lady come near to making a constant amity. But even there the poetic needs appear. Why is Britomart to be so highly in love with Artegal? Because she is to be the mother of the great lords of Britain, 'renowned kings, and sacred Emperors'. It is beautiful and thrilling, but it is no reason, nor is there any corresponding passion of reason, why Chastity should love Justice.

It seems, then, that Truth in this poem must be subordinated to, and in a sense annihilated by, Beauty. Intellectual perception, which in Pope had been divided by his genius, is here evaded; and when by chance it is present it is there rather as a fancy than a fact. Whatever the luxury of loveliness needs, must be provided at the expense of the pure abstract thought which has also been invoked, and the dark conceit is made doubly dark by its own forgetfulness. Abstractions have destroyed poetry often enough ; it is perhaps now but a fair revenge. In the process of poetry, however, it is worth noting that there is a parallel to this one-sidedness in another poem of Spenser's, the *Hymn to Heavenly Beauty*. In the conclusion of that imagination of the conclusion of all things all imaginable things are left behind.

Ne from thenceforth doth any earthly sense
Or idle thought of earthly things remain :
But all that erst seemed sweet, seems now offence,
And all that pleasèd erst now seems to pain.

He repents—so unnecessarily !—of the idle fancies
of his foolish thought, and will think of nothing
but

the love of God, which loathing brings
Of this vile world, and these gay seeming things.

It is a little hard on the vile world; one might go
farther and say that, though perhaps sanctity must
sometimes endure such a state for a season, it must
not, for poetry, nor indeed finally for sanctity, be
the conclusion. It was said of the God whom
Spenser was there hymning that He loved the world,
and certainly, whether the doctrine of the Resurrection be true or not, it seems only by some such
resurrection of the earth in their reconciled minds
that the poets can justly find union. 'All things have
second birth', wrote Wordsworth in a passionate
moment of the *Prelude*, and though he was there
speaking of the rhythms of existence in which even
destruction and massacre return, yet the maxim
seems to be a rule of poetry also. It was by no
process of exclusion that the genius of Shakespeare
proceeded. And the exclusion was a little ungrateful
in Spenser, who owed most of his poetry to the con-
taminating influence of the vile world, gay-seeming
things, and all the sweet that seemèd now offence.
But so it was. He abandoned earth, as he had abandoned the allegory, because he had not found identity.

VI

THE EVASION OF IDENTITY

(ii) THE *NIGHTINGALE* AND THE *GRECIAN URN*

I

THE *Nightingale* is by now accepted as one of the greatest aesthetic documents of English verse. But it may still be possible without superfluity to work on it a little, having in mind Marlowe's definition of the business of poetry. The effort which this Ode makes to express one inexpressible wonder of beauty is in the phrase 'rich to die' and in its relation of that phrase and state to the bird's song. To what poetic end is the suggestion of the deprivation of all experience turned into a rich experience? With that question as a beginning, it may be permissible once more to analyse the Ode itself, so as to reach the answer, if an answer exists, more certainly.

The poem opens with six important and correlated words—'aches', 'drowsy numbness', 'hemlock', 'opiate', 'Lethe'. They discover in us a sense of our capacity for sleep and death and oblivion. Whether we are conscious of it or not two other memories of hemlock are never far from the English imagination when the word is used—the cell of Athens and the gardens of Elsinore. Socrates is near, but the elder Hamlet and the poison entering 'the porches of his ears' are perhaps nearer. The memory of them encourages the lines to take us; a sleepy death is summoned.

But the next two lines, the fifth and sixth, define the sensation intellectually. It is not through envy, through a grudge at happiness which arises in a conscious unhappiness, but through an excess of happiness itself. The poet has entered into the felicity of the bird's enjoyment; hemlock and the opiate and Lethe are the details of 'being too happy', and that over-happiness is the awareness of a song with its own elements of detail—the light-winged Dryad, the trees, the melodious plot, the beechen green, the shadows, the song of summer, the full-throated ease. And immediately on those words the poem turns off to speak of wine. Why? Why does the thought of the beaker with beaded bubbles occur now? It is no doubt realistic enough, one might well wish for a draught of wine in those admirable circumstances, but natural logic in a great poem will have a poetic logic to support or perhaps to suggest it, and the poetic logic is here. The draught of wine corresponds to the earlier draught of hemlock; it even carries on the idea of full-throated. Indeed it is on that very word that the poem has turned. The bird's throat full of song becomes the poet's feeling the wine, and has therefore transmuted his hearing into the much closer experience of tasting. Taste is more immediate than sight or hearing, and drinking a more physically intimate thing than listening to a song. But though the change in the kind of experience suggested is deeper, we are still brought back again to the theme; only by that process, that introduction of the richer experience of wine, we are now easily introduced to new details of a similar kind to those of the first stanza, but themselves richer. Beechen green becomes country green; melodious plot becomes dance and Provençal song and sunburnt mirth, shadows numberless become the hinted dark of the deep-delvèd earth, and the Dryad has become the more mature and majestic Flora. And all these things in turn prepare us for an excursion—to the plot? or even the place of sunburnt mirth? no, but to a deeper richness of which the plot itself is but an open glade, to the forest dim. The bird's song is to fade away into *that*; the song and Keats and we are about to enter together into a grander and greater imagery.

But the third stanza delays us: in that already visioned forest we shall forget—what the poem will take care that we shall not yet forget. Eight lines are spent upon the things of which we are to be oblivious and that word forget takes us back to the first stanza with its Lethe and its envy that was not to be envy. Poetry is here, in the loveliest way, doing what our friends do when (and if) they say, 'I won't remind you—'; what, to take a classic example, St. Paul did in his letter to Philemon— 'howbeit I say not that thou owest me thine own self also'. It is clear that the poem is determined to remember 'what thou among the trees hast never known'. It will have leaden-eyed despairs, and Beauty's lustrous eyes all in it, youth and the passing of youth, love and dereliction of love. If it will not envy, at least it will tell us of all the causes for envy and it mingles its contradictions. Beauty has lustrous eyes and cannot keep them; but we are not to remember that she cannot. New love—even new love—cannot last more than a day, but we are not to remember that it cannot. So, echoing and re-echoing to the mind, so, sensibly distressing and sensibly soothing, the poem fades away into the forest dim.

Fades. But the next stanza abolishes so solemn and drowsy a departure. Twice in this poem the bird's song is to fade, and the second time, at the extreme close, it is to fade indeed, but that is far enough off at present. A different movement possesses us. As the first drowsy awareness had changed to the richer wine, and that in turn back again to the mightier knowledge of landscape and dim forests, so, by another metaphor of motion, the vision of landscape and forest is to change again. There had been a draught of vintage, yet there had not; there had only been a longing for it, and the longing is, in a sense, movement such as the stillness of the first stanza, even with its sinking Lethewards, had not been. Desire looks out; it includes in its naming of the thing desired the space or time of separation; it projects itself across separation. And now that recalled movement, stilled while we forget what we must not forget, becomes an intenser and swifter movement still. 'Fade' becomes 'fly to thee'; 'the beaker' becomes 'charioted by Bacchus and his pards'; the warm South is now the panthers of the very God. For the 'not' is there only in relation to the coming affirmation; it does not deny the panthers, it refuses them, and they must be there in order to be refused for something swifter, something more like the bird itself. The poem is to have wings as the Dryad had, though less seen yet heavier, for it has to remember and refuse now all those eight lines of unhappiness, which it does in seven words —'though the dull brain perplexes and retards'. In

that phrase the poem determined the kind of poem
it was going to be; it rejected the mind. It did so
here not in the least because of any contempt for
the mind, it is not a stupid mind. We have been
told why it is dull—because 'but to think is to be
full of sorrow And leaden-eyed despairs'. It is heavy,
itself perplexed and retarded, with its own proper
knowledge. It is dull with sorrow and despair.

And then, in one of the great Keats moments,
while the poem is still vibrating with 'away! away!'
while we are still almost in process of passing from
'with thee fade' to 'fly to thee', while that sudden
transmutation from passive consciousness to ardour
of movement through beauty is going on, the end
is there—'Already with thee!' And all that that
means, among which is another change from all with
which the poem began.

It began with a Dryad and beechen green and
hearing; it went on to Flora and country green and
drinking; it goes on to the Queen-Moon who is
herself left for verdurous glooms. The Queen-Moon
and her starry fays are part of the forest; before
Keats entered it they were not known. The forest
is the forest in which the queen of fairies and her
cluster of fays indeed existed when Shakespeare
discovered them by giving them mortal words, and
that is why they are there in Keats. For the identification of the moon and stars with fairy beings is
not a mere decoration; it gives the imagined beings
of the wood the royalty of the night, and by so doing
it brings the night and the wood into union. The
moon is unnamed, for here she is neither Titania nor
Dian but she is nearer Titania than Dian. There is

only one forest in English verse, in the more civilized parts of which a banished Duke lives with his people, and in deeper haunts Comus wanders with his rout, and elsewhere the lovers of Athens follow enchantment, and here a poet hears the nightingale. But the fays are starry: the night and the wood are one; the darkness is discovered within and not cast from without upon the verdurous glooms. As much as the melodious plot was less than they, so much less was the Dryad's song than that which is soon to be heard. But as we were to forget what we were caused to remember, so we are now to see and smell what we cannot see and smell. Keats can only guess because of the rich night, but he will see that we do more than guess.

The whole poem is full of these invocations and denials at once. It is its way of proceeding. It is concerned to find motives for banishing what it calls up and for recalling what it has banished. The Dryad is to be dismissed; the country goddesses fade before greater deities; the Queen-Moon is to show her light that she may make the darkness deeper, that—she being incapable of piercing this darkness with her light—it may be full of the smell of the balms. The vintage was richer than the song; but vintage is not a word for death and embalmed is. Hemlock has become hawthorn, but the mid-May's eldest child is still an opiate towards death.

Yet the drowsy numbness that sank towards Lethe has now become aware of Lethe, and of the elements that compose Lethe. Lethe, as in the old myth, is an actual thing, and oblivion is compact of analysable qualities. The shadows numberless which answered to the drowsy numbness have become the night in which Keats himself darkling listens. But the song continues; only, though the same, it is a different song.

Hemlock, opiate, Lethe—the opening of the poem had called Death soft names. It has been the business of poetry to use soft names; many a mused rhyme has in the lesser places of the art called so upon great experiences. 'Death is the end of woes; die soon, O faery's son.' But the viewless wings,[1] the art which is to remember and forget the immortal distresses of life, to bring them near and yet keep them far from the trees, are now to draw closer to an imagined experience. A possible sepulchre of embalmed darkness with incense of odours has been prepared; to die, to cease with no pain, to become a sod in those verdurous glooms—such an experience is all but imagined as happening. All but— it *seems* rich to die. Quite another kind of death, and other miseries similar to it, had been remembered in the third stanza, but they have been left behind. They are remembered but in contrast to this dream of a lovelier death. But perhaps their rejection is what keeps this death only a seeming, a dream, or if dream is too poor a word, let us say a rich vision; as rich as any could desire, as rich as this poetry could bear, but still an imagined vision and not an imagined actuality. For the dull brain also has been left behind, and the poem, perhaps

---

[1] The viewless wings of Keats are close to the viewless winds of Wordsworth. But Keats was thinking of flying to poetry as an escape from knowledge, and Wordsworth of poetry that was to become knowledge.

for that reason, pulsates on the moment of death, but does not enter it. Or let us go further, and use its own phrase; it is uncertain whether it sleeps or wakes. But the very greatest poetry always knows, and knows that it is awake.

There is in fact the smallest uncertainty, for all its incredible loveliness, about the next stanza, an uncertainty recognized in the last stanza, which is why we need not mind admitting what the poem itself exactly knew—'the fancy cannot cheat'. We may allow the hesitation over the Nightingale which has communicated itself to distinguished critics. But this intellectual hesitation is in the poem itself an emotional uncertainty; the evidence of it is in the single word 'perhaps', and in the fairy lands on which the stanza closes.

Keats, it has been said, thought of himself as dead and the nightingale as singing over him; he thought of many others who had died, generations trodden down by their successors, and by a natural if rationally incorrect process he went on to forget that nightingales also died, and to pretend that one nightingale sang to all the passing generations. The answer to that would be quite simple—we should say that Keats had imagined himself into a state where he heard not a nightingale but Nightingale, the archetypal and immortal bird: if it were not that the process of the stanza seems to be slightly but definitely away from so lofty an interpretation. For two lines the union of the two hemispheres of that imagination are achieved—the dead poet, the living song, and then it is no longer pure Nightingale that is present; it is a Nightingale

heard by Keats : that is, Keats has abandoned the
vision of himself as dead. He is living—not merely
in fact to write the poem, but in imagination in the
poem. 'The voice I hear this passing night'—why
'passing night' ? have we not heard that he wrote
the poem in the daytime ? We have and he did,
and are we to tie a poet so strictly to literal fact as
all that ? May he not have remembered the night ?
He may ; only the fact may encourage us for a
moment to believe that the night may have some
connexion with the tender night of stanza four in
which that high place of funeral had been prepared.
It is that night, that midnight when death was
almost felt to be present, when the sod that had
been Keats was to lie for ever in the verdurous ways
down which the song of the true Nightingale was
pouring—it is that night also which is passing. And
it is passing because Keats is still alive to hear with
his own attentiveness the song that had been heard
by similar listeners in the past—*perhaps* by Ruth.
And, consequently, perhaps not. But if not, then
certainly it is no more the archetypal song to which
we are listening.

It is perhaps not without significance that,
whether or not the words 'passing night' refer to
the mysterious night of the poem, still in them
movement has again recommenced, and that an
opposite movement. From the drowsy numbness
the movement of longing had brought us to the
contemplation of Flora, and then the movement of
passage to the forest, and in the forest movement
had ceased for the whole of the fifth and the opening of the sixth stanzas. Then there followed

complete absence and presence of movement at once,
but the presence was not of physical or temporal
movement, only the everlasting sound of the song.
But there is aroused another sense ; it *seemed* rich
to die ; it did but seem, and the night of that seeming is already on its way of departure.

We are then imagining ourselves back in Keats's
awareness, and we are there in the sense not merely
that we are reading his poem but that the poem
itself has returned to that as its subject, at least in
this stanza its intermittent subject. And therefore,
even in and for the poem, Keats is not dead. And
therefore, we are no more aware than he, living, can
be of the archetypal nightingale. Our knowledge
of his awareness increases.

> Thou wast not born for death, immortal Bird ;
> No hungry generations tread thee down—

Keats is not there.

> The voice I hear this passing night was heard
> In ancient days by emperor and clown—

He is there ; he is listening again.

> Perhaps the self-same song that found a path
> Through the sick heart of Ruth—

He is so much there that an element of uncertainty has entered. The alternative is to say that
he did not mean 'perhaps' ; he meant 'no doubt' or
'indeed'. But it is rash to play that kind of trick
with great verse ; we had better believe the Muse
was right when she taught him to say 'perhaps'[1].

[1] It has been suggested to me (the suggestion ought not to have
been needed) that the 'perhaps' covers the possibility that Ruth

And, incidentally, why Ruth ? Because Keats had been reading the Bible or Wordsworth, or because he thought of 'home' as a rhyme and then of 'sick for home', and then found a legendary figure who was so troubled. Or for any other such accidental reason. But in the poem she corresponds to something else ; she is there that she may incarnate a longing, the longing of the earlier stanzas, the longing for the wine and the longing for the forest. She is 'the impersonated thought, The idea or abstraction of (her) kind', and Keats was very certainly one of her kind. 'My heart aches . . . the sad heart.' Here then is Keats, listening in his own exile, seen in another image than himself, and the fact is certified to us by the little word 'alien'. So exquisitely does the poem follow its business which was not to imagine death and the archetypal world—save for those two lines—but to imagine the imagination of it, that in the word it renews its own proper purpose. It is a word of one kind and not of the other, a word of our knowledge of Ruth, not of pure Ruth. 'Sad heart . . . sick for home . . . stood in tears', that is Ruth ; but 'alien corn' is not Ruth, her sad heart never conceived the alien, the learned, the curious word. 'Strange', even 'foreign' she might have said, but never 'alien'.

This, however, it will be justly observed, is subjective criticism given its head, and that part of the argument is not necessary. The main fact is that by the time we are done with Ruth we are entirely back with Keats. We are swept on into another

heard either no song or that (say) of the lark. It is possible, but I do not much believe Keats meant it so.

world, as if we were returning by the same road we took to the centre of those verdurous glooms; we are back in faery, as if the starry fays of the excluded light returned to shine upon perilous seas. The poem has here no time for, or knowledge of, the gods, as it had earlier. The nightingale's song has charmed a magical world, with forlorn lands, and the poem wakes forlorn to hear the song itself dying.

Is it the first nightingale or the second that is fading? Both, but rather the first, for the second is lost when the long journey is retraced in nine words, 'toll me back from thee to my sole self'. 'The fancy cannot cheat.' It had seemed to the poem rich to die, but because it stopped there and did not fully imagine that death it could only seem to itself to be rich. The great experiences of death and possession ('having nothing, yet possessing all things') were not for it. Can it be that, desiring them, it ought not so swiftly to have fled from the dull brain ?

II

The *Ode on the Grecian Urn* was written before the *Nightingale* and might be considered as an introduction to it. It is concerned with a related, but not identical, experience; the difference between the two is double—first, in the final experience imagined and conveyed ; second, in the means of approach to it, which is also part of either poem. This means of approach in the *Nightingale* conceived itself as obliged to abandon the 'dull brain' ; there was (we are told) no place for it until in the last stanza the

mused rhyme began to return and provided an intellectual judgement upon the whole experience.
But the *Urn* pretends to allow more space to intellect ; only in its last stanza does it accede to a
similar renunciation, only there is it 'teased out of
thought'. The physical sense which it imagines in
action is more consonant with thought, for sight is
more prolonged and distant than the taste to which
the *Nightingale* transformed its earlier hearing, and
than the whole remarkable world which the later
hearing created after that double transformation.
Sight allows opportunity for contemporary thought,
and teased out of thought though the poem eventu-
ally declares itself to be, its final declaration is very
like an intellectual statement. 'Beauty is truth, truth
beauty'; it is a statement both by and about the intellect, though certainly induced by the sensations
as well. One of the terms is the object of all intellectual labour. Yet it has been teased out of thought
before it makes that statement.

The *Nightingale* imagines the poet as undergoing,
at first, the experience of an organic and changing
thing ; the *Urn* of an inorganic and unchanging
thing. The *Nightingale*, it is true, proceeds to
something like the imagination of an organic and unchanging thing : there, even more truly than in the
Urn, it might be said that never 'can those trees be
bare', nor can the bird leave its song. In some sense
the great stanzas of the *Nightingale* awake the knowledge of the living state, the inorganic image of which
had been the cause of the envy in the *Urn*. For
there is envy there, and not movement, though the
envy disappears in the last stanza, subdued by a

gnomic wisdom. But the difference in kind of the two poems is in their use of the word 'ecstasy'. 'What wild ecstasy?' 'In such an ecstasy.' The one inquires; the other experiences. Strictly in the *Urn* the inquiry is not answered. But indirectly it is answered by the invocation of the figures, they are imagined to know something unattainable by man —the Beauty that keeps her lustrous eyes, the love that pines at them beyond to-morrow: 'for ever wilt thou love and she be fair.'

They are imagined to know it, but only by a contradiction, a contradiction implicit in the whole of the *Urn*, from its first exquisite expression at the opening of the second stanza. Heard melodies are sweet, but (rationally speaking) unheard melodies are not sweeter—they are not sweet at all for they are to have 'no tone'. That which has no tone is sweeter than that which has tone. This is either the avowal of a profound negation, or it is a contradiction.[1] All that is said of the figures on the urn pursues that contradiction. They are apostrophized as living because they are not living, for if indeed they lived it could only be in a world of unlustrous Beauty, and that is the world we are to desert. The silent form reveals sensuous joys; the cold pastoral perpetuates warmth, enjoyment, and a panting heart. But only because it never can become them. The poem makes that contradiction a part of itself; it refuses the intellect as the *Nightingale* abandons

[1] The sweetness of heard melodies may disappoint us; we may be aware of unfulfilled potentialities of sweetness in the imagined melody. But I do not think they are fulfilled to the inner any more than to the outward ear.

the intellect. 'The dull brain . . . teased out of thought.'

As the slightest note of uncertainty is heard in the archetypal song and the fancy is sorrowfully admitted to fail in its deception, so here the moral of the end is shaken by all that preluded it. 'Beauty is truth, truth is beauty', but we have had to abandon intellectual truth in order to reach that state; we have had, so wonderfully, to pretend. And if it is only by means of pretence we can find that

> that is all
> Ye know on earth and all ye need to know,

how can we use the word 'truth' at all ?

To say so much of these two poems is not in the least to depreciate or discredit them. A poem is no less a poem because it expresses one state of things rather than another; only we ought to be clear what state of things it is expressing. The poems themselves admit their nature to the full; the *Urn* allows that it is cheating, the *Nightingale* (of a more advanced experience) laments that it cannot cheat. They both desire conclusion, reconciliation, union, fullness of experience, the state where 'Beauty is truth, truth is Beauty', where the complete satisfaction of sensation is the complete satisfaction of exalted reason. But the one avoids the integrity of reason as the other avoids the sensation of death. And perhaps because they do both avoid, because they live, as poems, only by avoiding, we are left still a little discontented. There remains still a wonder expressed. How even yet is poetry to discover that union of which it has had visions ? how are the Arab's stone and shell to be one? and a full amplitude of mind to find its absolute power?

III

In *Lamia*, at least, Keats might be held to have gone a step farther, both in doing it and in discovering how it was and was not to be done. For having allowed the *Urn* to tease him out of thought and the archetypal song to lure him away from the mind, he went back on his steps in that later poem and caused Philosophy to destroy both sensuous beauty and (as a consequence) the lover of sensuous beauty. Apollonius in *Lamia* is certainly by way of being a rather austere philosopher, but since it was presumably he who taught Lycius Plato, it was rather his own temper than the necessity of Philosophy which made him so. Plato himself was the last philosopher to 'clip an angel's wings', and it is Platonism which has given Lycius his 'uneager' face. It is a question how far we are to take the Platonism seriously; 'the calm'd twilight of Platonic shades' is hardly a sufficient description of a world from which the nightingale's song is a truer derivation. But whether Keats is responsible for the misreading or whether he meant it as a description of the false peace which Lycius thinks he has achieved does not perhaps very much matter. Lycius throws Apollonius over in favour of Beauty—rather like Keats in the two odes; indeed Lycius has decided that for him Beauty—Lamia's beauty—is sufficient truth. Lamia herself is more than willing to fill this part, only Lycius is anxious to assert his creed before the world, and make rather a boast of it. He falls into a 'mad pom-

pousness', and alarmed Beauty has to make the best
she can of it. She does her best; her 'doubtful ser-
vitors' adorn the palace. She puts out all her power:
what will philosophy do against this? All that philosophy need do; it merely looks at it unsympatheti-
cally. It looks, one might say, at the Grecian Urn,
both the thing and the poem, and the beautiful
fancies by which the carven lovers were thought to
be living perish. In fact, Lamia perishes before
Apollonius because she had taken on a nature which
was not hers, and could not therefore sustain the
penetrating gaze of intellect. Keats introduced the
rainbow as a simile.

> There was an awful rainbow once in heaven:
> We know her woof, her texture; she is given
> In the dull catalogue of common things.

But if the Beauty of the rainbow depends for its
effectiveness on our *not* knowing its woof and texture,
if to know the actual identity of any apparent loveliness is to destroy it, of what worth—even poetically
—can that loveliness actually be? It depends on a
point of view; it depends on keeping something
out. And what use is any imagination in the end
that depends on keeping something out? It was
not Marlowe's teaching. And can even imagination
keep that something out? No more than Lamia's
prayer or Lycius' discourtesy could keep out Apollonius; equally discourteous, he came. It was as
much his nature and business to see the serpent as
it was the serpent's nature and business to take
advantage of the presence of a God to turn herself
into a woman and a capacity to lure Lycius from

Plato; in fact, to fulfil her own nature as Apollonius fulfilled his. They fulfilled themselves; they destroyed each other, and the end of the poem is death. Neither this Beauty nor this Reason can abandon their own natures, and the result is 'the universe of death', which Wordsworth had told us was the opposite of 'the world of life' in which the great minds exist.

But it is, of course, a world of life in which the persons of the poem have existed, and even their death is part of it. It is rich to us that they should die; so far at least the mutations of Keats's mind had been sent abroad. He had destroyed Lamia as effectively and inevitably as Spenser had caused Sir Guyon to trample the gardens of Acrasia; and without (so far as we can see) the same excuse. For at least the prisoner of Acrasia had been redeemed while the victim of Lamia and Apollonius is dead. Keats in the passage on the rainbow had seemed to associate himself with Lycius against Apollonius; he had preferred the mere seeming to the actual identity of the thing, as he had done in the *Urn*. It was, however, as we very well know, only his method of finding his own process. It was the *Nightingale* method, the method of the dreamer, which the *Fall of Hyperion* rejected; had it not been for his concern with the miseries of the world the Keats of that poem would have perished before he touched the steps of the altar. The forgotten and remembered miseries of the *Ode to a Nightingale* saved him. Even the *Melancholy* rejects the *Nightingale* in two phrases: 'Lethewards had sunk'—'No, no, go not to Lethe'; 'a drowsy numbness pains'—'shade to

shade will come too drowsily"[1]. It had indulged itself, however, in the second stanza, though it corrected its error in the last. The mistress whose hand
was imprisoned had still left that hand imprisoned.
But the third stanza forsook her. Beauty is to die
—even the peerless eyes of that mistress are not to
keep their lustres. Even the beauty of the *Nightingale*
perhaps is to die; certainly we are returning to the
world of knowledge which there we had rejected.
Greater poets than Keats entered the sovran shrine
of Melancholy, but they found there trophies no
longer clouded but terribly distinct. They recognized the forms and substances of very Melancholy,
and shaped a conceit of the separation of Beauty
and Truth.

[1] It even—but that is fantasy—refuses the owl of Spenser, and
it does not yet know of the owl of *Macbeth*; it can but forbid
'the downy owl' to be 'a partner in your sorrow's mysteries'.

VII

'A LADY'S EYES'

IT was said that Shakespeare in Berowne's speech on love defined it as giving 'to every power a double power', and we may remember Wordsworth's continual use of the word 'power' in relation to poetry. Wordsworth also attributed this increase of power to love, though he was talking about a rather more advanced state of that much misunderstood capacity than Berowne. He said it came— this power—from a process by which fear was ended in love, and that love caused intercourse with the adverse principles of pain and joy. He added that this love could not act or exist without Imagination which was another name for absolute power.

Love is so dangerous and difficult a word that it is good to escape from Wordsworth's spiritual sublimities back to more normal experience, back to Berowne and *Love's Labour's Lost*. There is no doctrinal, no philosophical hypothesis, in Shakespeare; what change there is in him is in his style and only in his style. Berowne's allocution is about a love which his friends and we understand very well—it is 'love first learnèd in a lady's eyes'. Still, Berowne goes on to say that it is this love which is set free from the brain where it has been rather uselessly confined and set free to skim about the various functions and capacities of a lover. The emotions as well as the mind are awakened, power is redoubled, and the power is set free to write, which otherwise it would never dare do. It will not be wise to say that

this is the only method; though Wordsworth, it will
be remembered, was similarly thrilled into his sense
of dedication as a poet. But it is certainly the method
with which the earlier work of Shakespeare was
chiefly concerned.

Setting aside the historical plays, it seems to be
true that beauty in those earlier plays is largely
identified with women's beauty. It is from the eyes
of the ladies in the comedies and *Romeo* that love is
born, and it is in the light of their eyes that for long
he happily plays. Sometimes, of course, the world
destroys it, but only when it destroys the mother as
well. There is not, I think, right up to *Hamlet* a
woman who for good or bad reasons abandons the
love which is her child. Men do, either from light-
ness or under enchantment or by compulsion, but
not women. This, of course, proves nothing at all,
except that it leaves the sense of beauty in women
more of an integral beauty than it would otherwise
have been, for all those separate beauties confirm
and encourage each other—Luciana, Bianca, Julia,
Silvia, the Princess and her ladies, Juliet, Hermia,
and Helena, Portia and Nerissa and Jessica, Rosa-
lind and Celia, Olivia and Viola. They all talk the
most lovely poetry about love, and we never have to
feel that because of their actions it is perhaps not
quite so simple as all that. Even the queens and
ladies of the historical plays are allowed to be devoted
to their own husbands or causes; even Tamora is
devoted to Aaron. Queen Margaret certainly has
her intimate friendship with Suffolk, but after all
she had been married to him as proxy (consider
Guenevere !), and when he had been killed she grew

fierce for her husband's rights, and anyhow perhaps
Shakespeare didn't plot out 2 *Henry VI*! Their love-
poetry is integral to their love, and that to their
beauty; 'beauty is truth, truth beauty'. And the
result of that is that all the faculties are sharpened
to discern actualities (so Berowne tells us). It is not
till we come to Gertrude that we begin to consider
change and alteration, and the whole matter there
is confused by Hamlet's violent antagonism to her
second marriage. Just occasionally one wishes that
Gertrude had stood up to her son, and told him to
mind his own business. For really when one comes
to consider, in cold blood, the language he uses to
her because she married again rather quickly—yes,
but one never can consider it in cold blood for there
is nothing to consider but the language which pre-
vents the blood from waiting on the judgement. It
is a magnificent piece of insolence on Shakespeare's
part to tell us solemnly about the heyday in the blood
being tame and humble, when he is so working it
up that we all agree that Gertrude may have been
guilty of adultery and possibly privy to murder when
there is little enough to suggest it! Gertrude is
not presented as Beauty, the mother of love, nor
Claudius as a romantic lover; and Ophelia is—perhaps deliberately—pushed out of the way of any
action at all. So that, by and large, we are not disturbed in our sense of the integrity of beauty, though
Hamlet is given poetry which expresses his own
sense of its collapse.

Keats had committed himself to his assertion
when, rejecting the integrity of the mind, he had
stared at that Greek urn on which the Greek lovers

were engraved. By the chance of poetry it was a
Greek scene also in which Shakespeare now proceeded to imagine two lovers who are the precise
contrary of Keats's lovers, and also (which is the
present point) to carry the intellect also, to carry
reason, into this imagination. I have elsewhere discussed the possible relation of *Troilus and Cressida*
to the whole development of Shakespeare's genius.[1]
This essay is concerned with what Shakespeare chose
to do with reason at that point. At last, after so
many plays, we are to have one in which beauty and
truth are not integral to the mind. It is, I think,
necessary to realize that the question of Cressida is
not seriously raised at all. Shakespeare does not say
she was right or wrong ; he gives her her own nature
and lets her get on with it. Thersites and Ulysses
are critical of her, but neither Thersites nor Ulysses
are Shakespearian judges. Ulysses' wisdom indeed
is definitely unsuccesful in its stratagems. It is Troilus and the effect on Troilus over which Shakespeare
is taking all his trouble. It is Troilus who says, in so
many words, 'O withered truth !' and 'O beauty !
where is thy faith ?' For neither Troilus nor Cressida had been imagined as carved upon an urn. They
were not static beauty but beauty in movement,
capable of change.

They had been in propinquity ; they had been in
love ; they had been anxious to maintain that love's
identity—at least, Troilus had and Cressida had
sweetly permitted herself to conjoin with him. This
last presumably is what is meant by truth—that of
which the identity everlastingly exists. Outside that,

[1] *The English Poetic Mind.* Oxford, 1932.

truth can have but a speculative meaning for us.
If beauty cannot keep her lustrous eyes nor new love
weep at them, then, to that extent, truth has ceased
to exist. The change may be a fact, and truth may
be the fact of change. But then it has lost its identity
with the original beauty; it may, of course, have
another, but that we shall have to find out.

They had been in propinquity, and Shakespeare
first of all destroyed that propinquity, or found he
had chosen a tale which did destroy it. He eased
the change for us then as he did not afterwards.
Othello had something worse to put up with, and
we, watching him, have to imagine something worse.
It is partly Troilus' own fault, and partly Ulysses',
that he suffers; we cannot blame him for eaves-
dropping, but we must admit that he does—as
any one and every one in the circumstances would.
He could hardly be expected to appreciate Shakespeare's thoughtfulness in removing Cressida from
Troy before she was allowed to become fully 'a
daughter of the game'; nor, in fact, did he. *Romeo
and Juliet* had found its conclusion in some such
enforced parting; and Shakespeare gave to the
parting of the Trojan lovers such a sweetness as
seems briefly to sum up *Romeo and Juliet*, before he
passed on to a separation the Veronese had never
known. Nor had foreseen; they urged no constancy
upon each other. But Troilus is urgent for that
constancy and truth, and yet—ever so slightly—
fears there is something which may prevent it,
something almost in the nature of things.

Troilus.   But be not tempted.
Cressida. Do you think I will?

Troilus.   No,
    But something may be done that we will not:
    And sometimes we are devils to ourselves
    When we will tempt the frailty of our powers,
    Presuming on their changeful potency.

The 'something may be done that we will not' looks forward to the greater catastrophes which, in *Othello* and *Lear*, were to follow on a lesser actual cause. Cressida, again, is potential of change. It is doubtful whether Troilus goes altogether the best way to avert change, but that too was in his nature and could not be helped.

And change is not averted. Beauty is, quite finally for Troilus, not truth; beauty has lost her soul. Shakespeare's imagination has proceeded to the discovery of a state where Keats's maxim is contradicted by experience, but the real anguish is that the maxim is present in order to be contradicted. He had discovered one thought, one wonder which has not been digested into words. Beauty caused suffering to Troilus as to Tamburlaine, and of the same kind.

    I am giddy, expectation whirls me round.
    The imaginary relish is so sweet
    That it enchants my sense. What will it be
    When that the watery palate tastes indeed
    Love's thrice-repured nectar? death, I fear me,
    Swounding destruction, or some joy too fine,
    Too subtle-potent, tun'd too sharp in sweetness
    For the capacity of my ruder powers.

This is very much the 'conceit of foil' of Marlowe. But now the conquest of that beauty has involved

Shakespeare in imagining and Troilus in experiencing a different kind of defeat. It is a defeat which
attacks his whole being, and in his being his reason.
He feels he will 'lie in publishing a truth'. He is
prepared to deny that Cressida was there, and 'my
negation hath no taste of madness'. This denial then
is reasonable. A denial of the known facts is reasonable : that is, 'reason can revolt Without perdition'.
On the other hand, the facts are known, and must
therefore be reasonable ; 'loss assume(s) all reason,
Without revolt'. This is the 'madness of discourse'
set up by its cause—though Shakespeare does not
use the pronoun ; he refers to 'cause' simply : 'that
cause sets up with and against itself'. The bi-fold
authority which now exists is a bi-fold authority of
Reason.

It is a division and contradiction expressed in the
idiom of Shakespeare : the idiom of human beings,
of handsome young men, beautiful young women,
and love. But though it is his idiom, it has been the
language of our general poetic mind. Marlowe has
expressed the continual preoccupation, and declared
that however high poetry goes there will always be
some beauty unexpressed, which nevertheless it is
the business and nobility of the poets to attempt to
express. Wordsworth has declared that Reason is an
element in the highest poetry, the passionate and
sublime reason by which all things are related in
power. Pope used Reason, to his degree, in two
different ways : the discursive Reason of my lord
Bolingbroke's mind, and the intuitive reason of his
own Nihilistic genius. Spenser sought to combine
Reason and Beauty : truth allegorized into loveli-

ness. But truth faded beneath the loveliness, and at the last indescribable pitch of heavenly beauty all describable earthly beauty, and therefore for poetry all beauty, found itself forgotten. Keats, at any rate in the *Nightingale* and the *Urn*, preferred to abolish earthly suffering; to leave it behind with the 'dull brain' or to be 'teased out of thought' and out of earthly reason, in order to be free to assert that 'beauty was truth, truth beauty', and to experience imagined death under the imagined song. But something failed; the song faded, for the death was not, after all, death. And the genius of Keats himself was hardly satisfied : *Lamia* and *Hyperion* and the *Melancholy* point to some other way. Beauty had been truth in Shakespeare through many a felicity and infelicity of love, until he chose to express a conceit that Marlowe had not formed and an actuality that Keats had put behind for a while—the disintegration of beauty and truth in the mind of a believer (let us for a moment imagine—as if in a lesser Keats), and found that reason itself seemed to have disintegrated under the strain.

What, after such a discovery, can poetry do? *Solvitur dicendo*; what it has done, and what more in the future it may do. But in the past it has done chiefly two things, and those by the two imaginations of Milton and Shakespeare. It has, in the one, imagined that 'madness of discourse' as subordinated to Reason ; it has imagined a sublime Reason in control of the universe, a Reason which is at the same time absolute Power; and this controlling 'truth and beauty' it has imagined in relation to the contending and contradicting states of divided souls.

But in the other, it has followed the 'madness of discourse' itself, abandoning—at least explicitly— the divine Reason, and tracing the conflict deeper and deeper until in some sense it has imagined earth, under the influence of the operation of false-hood, ravening upon itself. It has traced the path of destruction.

VIII

THE DEIFICATION OF REASON

It is a remarkable fact that even distinguished critics still sometimes talk about the inhumanity of Milton; they imply that the imagination which created *Paradise Lost* is in no sort of relation to human experience, beyond the experience of *Paradise Lost* as a highly effective technical achievement. For us, it seems, Milton has created ten thousand lines of greatness about nothing at all. At most we may be allowed to have some sense of recognition of Satan's defeat and defiance; for the rest we are to enjoy the many little descriptive touches, such as 'the Chineses', which Milton deigned to put in, and the marvellous subtlety of the infinite variations of the decasyllabic line.

If that were so we should have to revise our idea of great poetry, or to deny that Milton was a great poet; and when we say Milton here we mean *Paradise Lost*. The earlier stuff we are allowed to keep; we are even permitted *Samson*. It is the *Paradises* that all the fuss is about, especially the first. *Paradise Regained*, being mainly an argument, can afford to be inhuman. But *Paradise Lost* is a story and yet inhuman. There is, fortunately, an alternative; it may be merely superhuman. It is so easy to think that great poetry is, in itself, what at the moment we are. But it may be more. It may be a fact that *Paradise Lost* is difficult to us because Milton's imagination is so much more than ours, that in fact he is a great poet. He may have made slips;

he may have failed sometimes. But he may be a great poet for all that.

It is, of course, a thing almost impossible to prove, because of the nature both of the problem and the proof. It was comparatively easy for Addison to prove that, by all the rules of art, *Paradise Lost* was an epic poem. Nobody nowadays cares whether it is an epic, properly so called, or not. But how can any one prove that the lines of the poem are effective, when his opponent has merely to deny? The present effort, therefore, can only pretend to make a few shy suggestions (denying its tempestuous heart).

Those suggestions may be summed up as follows: (i) that *Paradise Lost* is read too often only as a narrative and not sufficiently as a psychological poem; (ii) that the actual nature of the theme—which is announced to be disobedience and obedience—is not sufficiently observed, nor the nature of that obedience; (iii) that the despair of Satan and the pathos of Adam and Eve are regarded as the important achievements of Milton's imagination, whereas in fact it is the transcending of that despair and pathos which is his sublimity; (iv) that that sublimity consists—precisely as Wordsworth said it did—in an exaltation of Power, Reason, and Beauty; and in the use of his verse to express at once that Power, Reason, and Beauty, and all revolts against it with their adequate and inevitable conclusion.

(i) *Paradise Lost* is a narrative poem. It tells a story and it proceeds with that story throughout. But that story is not directly told. It begins with Satan in hell, brings him to earth, introduces God

nd heaven, and afterwards Adam and Eve; then it
ᴣcedes into the past, and recounts the fall of Satan,
nd the creation of the world; returns to the present,
nd concentrates on the Fall and the immediate
ᴣsults of the Fall; proceeds into the future and
ʌvolves the history of the world up to the Redemp-
on; then returns again to the present and describes
ɪe exile from Eden. There are many admirable
ᴣchnical reasons for this—at least, we can invent
ɪany. The narrative becomes a more complex
ɪing, and a more complete thing, since the original
'all and the final Redemption are more subtly in-
olved in its unity. But at the beginning of this
arrative Milton took a tremendous risk, for he
resented the defiant Satan in hell. On balance, he
as probably lost ever since by taking that risk, for
ɪe opening with all later phrases appertaining to
: has been remembered, treasured, believed, and
ometimes misapplied. But at least we may conclude
hat he took this risk deliberately; that he opened
ʌith Satan in hell because he wanted to open with
atan in hell; that the poem demanded this and no
ther beginning and got it.

From such an opening our whole awareness of
atan begins, and that awareness does not, as the
arrative does, return and double upon itself; it
oes directly on. Everything that follows has to
onfirm or correct, enlarge or diminish, stabilize or
ᴅestroy, and in every case analyse that impression.
Ʌhen, in the Fifth Book, we are told by Raphael
ʌhat was the original beginning of the whole matter,
hat account of Satan's earlier activity is imposed for
ɪs on our existing knowledge of his later behaviour.

The first presentation, however, has so often stupe-
fied us all that we do not allow ourselves to be affected
by the other later. But the result of our stupe-
faction is that Satan remains for us a magnificent
but a simple figure, whereas in fact, he is by no
means a simple figure. A second result is that we
are less apt to feel Milton's imagination rejecting
Satan, and the whole poem becomes disproportionate.
At the beginning Milton put out all but his whole
strength and created Satan. He heaped up all the
details of defeat and anguish, the 'dungeon horrible',
'the seat of desolation, void of light', 'the burning
marl' and the rest; against those he cast up the un-
defeated spirit of Satan; and against that he reared
the rest of the poem, which towers over Satan as
the gate of Eden at the close towers over the depart-
ing figures of our first parents.

As a mere narrative this effort might have failed,
and has been held to have failed, otherwise we
should not so entirely have equated the poetic effect
of *Paradise Lost* with the poetic effect of Satan. But
the experience of *Paradise Lost* is not merely the
experience of a narrative poem nor of Satan. It is
the experience of a psychological poem; nor is it
only the experience of Satan, but rather of that whole
psychological state in which Satan is a contrasting
and contending element. *Paradise Lost* is a universal
fabric of the imagination; its intensities are intensities of the spirit of man. For that reason Keats
was able to say of it, 'It grows a greater wonder
every day'. It is not Keats's experience alone,
though it may have been his, because of his genius,
in a greater measure than it is ours.

One indication of this content of the poem is in
the opening of the Third Book. Milton, speaking
of his own blindness, is invoking the heavenly light,
the light that shines inward and irradiates the mind
as the Spirit of the opening of the First Book preferred 'before all temples the upright heart and pure'.
That Spirit had been entreated in the First Book
to supply the poem with necessary genius, and to
justify in it the ways of its God. The inward shin-
ing light is now similarly besought to irradiate and
purge the mind, to disperse the mists,

> that I may see and tell
> Of things invisible to mortal sight.

These things are certainly the narrative of the
heavenly war and the original sin. But it seems
possible that they may also be the everlasting spiritual war and the continual sin, as Milton conceived
them. The attention is directed inward: the 'things
invisible' are the interior state of man. It is from
the habitual experiences of the soul of man that
Paradise Lost is constructed; the daily incidents of
the mind are here recognized 'in flashes and with
glory not their own'.

But the 'things invisible' must mean the theme
of the poem, and the relation of the persons to the
theme of the poem. 'The upright heart' of man is
the habitation of the Spirit of the poem; it would
not be surprising if the poem therefore were about
the habitation in which the Spirit that infuses it
preferred to dwell, if that habitation were in part
its theme, and if the obedience or disobedience
which is announced to be its theme were in relation
to the heart of man. The dispersed mist leaves

clear to us not merely the conflict in heaven before creation, but the conflict in the spirit after creation. All the persons also have this double state. It is not an allegory which we are studying, but an identity. But the identity is that of facts which belong to two categories—historical and contemporary, angelic and mortal, narrative and psychological, at once. It is by the theme of the poem that their double nature is made clear.

(ii) At the very beginning Milton preludes on this theme—it is to be 'man's first disobedience'. In the excitement of discussing the prosody of that line we have perhaps a little neglected the word 'disobedience'. Man was placed in Eden with two capacities—of obedience and of domination. He was to obey God's will, but also he was to be lord 'of the world beside'. There was, as Adam (having so little to talk about) explained to Eve, one sign of their obedience and many signs of their rule. Satan, who is in revolt against Reason, overhearing this, remarks that the prohibition is 'reasonless'. But Satan was perhaps no more the best judge than Troilus of Cressida. The Almighty explained it another way. Man is to know himself and to be known by others as man; that is, as a being at once in subordination and lordship; he is to know himself as this in the free exercise of his choice. Milton went so far as to say that Reason was choice, and in the unfallen state presumably it was; man obeyed his intellect. His intellect told him he ought to be inferior and superior at once, hierarchically exercising his double knowledge of the state in which he had been created. In the poem, it must be

remembered, Adam and Eve have no doubt at all
about God : they are not in our own extremely
hazy moral and metaphysical state. They know
themselves, and that they know themselves in relation to the Tree of Knowledge is but a proof—to
themselves as to all other uncreated and created
beings—that they know themselves rightly. Obedience is to them a positive experience of joy ; a fact
so incredible to us that we have refused it to them.
But it is to be between them and the Almighty a
means of delight, in the exquisite interchange of
corresponding will. It is (the Almighty remarks—
quite rightly) the only method by which he can
praise his creatures ; if they are not to be allowed to
choose, neither can they enjoy his will nor he theirs.
We now may naturally wish that he did not want to
enjoy our wills, but the regret had not then arisen.

This combination of subordination and lordship
is the state in which Adam and Eve exist ; it is
repeated between them. Eve derives delight from
her submission to Adam. Milton may have been
all wrong about that, though even there it is to be
noticed that he is talking about Adam and Eve in
a state of love and joy. It is Eve in a state of raptu-
rous delight with Adam who declares that he is her
law ; later on, when she was out of love, she was by
no means so clear about it, and only when a mutual
penitence and a mutual pardon has reunited them in a
renewed passion is Eve again subordinated to her lord.
It is not woman being inferior to man; it is a woman
finding delight in submitting to a man: a man, incidentally, who is in a state when he thinks that 'Wisdom in discourse with her Loses discountenanced

and like folly shows'. Milton's principles of the relations of the sexes may have been all wrong— probably because any principle of the relations of the sexes will be wrong, since there are, after all, no such things; there are an infinite number of women and an infinite number of men. The Lord Viscount St. Alban pointed out long ago that Plato mixed up his physics with his theology, and fell into error thereby. 'The sexes' is a convenient phrase, but misleading. Milton may, however, have been wrong in his general principles. But it is by no means so certain that he was wrong in his description of the psychological state of a woman—even of some women—passionately in love. Might not quite a number exclaim in that lovely state of joyous adoration:

> My Author and Disposer, what thou bidd'st
> Unargued I obey?

But of course, Milton, being inhuman, knew nothing of what a woman in love feels like. Let us return to the question of obedience.

Obedience is the means by which Adam and Eve know themselves for what they truly are. But it is also the means by which Satan and all the angels know themselves for what they truly are. Raphael explained that to us, in case we need to know (as apparently we do).

> Myself and all th' angelic host that stand
> In sight of God enthron'd, our happy state
> Hold, as you yours, while our obedience holds;
> On other surety none; freely we serve,
> Because we freely love, as in our will
> To love or not; in this we stand or fall.

Any one who has ever begun to envisage the
nature and experience of love might, one would
think, have recognized in those sublime words the
poetic discovery of a simple fact of that experience.
It is, surely, common knowledge that in proportion
as man freely loves—*loves*—he finds himself in a
state of stability. I do not say it is the only state;
only that it is a mark of that particular passion,
once known in the pure clarity in which it is here
described. The angels are angels—in the narrative.
But in the complex psychology of the universal poem,
they are man achieving for a moment a realization
of himself as free; they renew the idea of service
which, once known, is by its very nature freedom.
'In this we stand or fall.' But the fall is a matter
of experience, not merely of doctrine or legend.
Man rejecting this lucidity of obedience to love
falls into a state which has been earlier analysed in
the great Niphates speech and is again soon to
be described. The later description is at the close
of the Sixth Book, which is another exploration of
known experience. The spirit, angelic or human,
which refuses love, discovers Love destroying him.
Everything shakes within him, except for that single
centre of destructive power. He loses resistance to
that which was once nourishment and is now desolation; he loses courage to resist. He falls into a
collapse before it; it has in fact become an evil to
him; and its presence leaves him 'exhausted, spiritless, afflicted, fallen'. This, in the actual history,
has preceded Satan's Niphates choice of evil, but it
is the psychological sequence to it. 'Evil, be thou
my Good', says the Fourth Book; in the Sixth Good

is shown as having become evil to the spirits that so determined. Those spirits fall into something which the universal testimony of mankind has called something very like hell: 'hell at last Yawning received them whole'.

If this is what is meant by Milton's inhumanity, then Milton's inhumanity is the most extraordinarily exact description of the state of most men who refuse their wills to the power of a known love in its purity that any English poet ever found. But he presented it indirectly—(i) as a myth, (ii) in terms of obedience rather than emotional desire. He may, conceivably, have been right; we may have to know love as a state of obedience rather than of emotional desire. Milton was no easy romantic; he was a realist of the finest kind. And perhaps that is why he seems so unsentimentally inhuman.

Obedience has its sign, for otherwise it could not be known to either mortals or angels; you cannot know a thing if there is no way by which it can be known. And in order that Adam and Eve and Raphael and Satan may know themselves rightly they must know themselves in obedience, in the free love of facts as they are. It must be admitted that facts may not be as they are presented in *Paradise Lost*. There may be no God, no angels, and no obedience. Milton adopted a hypothesis, as all religious poets must do. But he made that hypothesis as interiorly exact to a great part of man's experience as ever hypothesis was made. Its least successful part is when Milton tries to present the operation of Redemption towards the end of the poem; perhaps even Milton found it difficult to imagine

THE DEIFICATION OF REASON   101

Redemption. But in the earlier part he has expressed
not merely the imagined alternative to the 'madness
of discourse', but even (and inevitably) the cause of
Troilus's distress. Whatever Troilus had been doing
he had not been freely loving; he had been impos-
ing conditions on his love, and very nearly boring
Cressida with his conditions. In the fallen state of
man, and aware as we are that we want—perhaps
rightly—other things besides free love, we may be
right to condition love, and Troilus may have been
right. But that conditioning was the cause of his
trouble; that and the fact (which was in him the same
fact) that he was not for God only. He was quite a
lot for Troilus. He was extraordinarily anxious about
Cressida's obedience to—to what he called love. But
he meant well. So did Othello. Milton has swept
away from these 'meaning wells'; he is making poetry
out of the pure choice, with all mists dispersed, or is
as near making poetry out of it as any poet can be.
The pure choice itself is inconceivable by man. But
Milton expressed three exquisitely analysed and syn-
thesized results, Satan, Adam, Christ.

(iii) To these first two points we shall return in
a consideration of the fourth; meanwhile, there is
the third, which is but the reverse of the fourth. I
have elsewhere commented on Milton's capacity
for imagining a fact intensely and then rejecting it
by a greater sweep of his imagination, in an allusion
to Adam's romantic devotion to Eve. Milton's inhumanity did not prevent him exploring, in the
power, reason, and beauty of his verse the passion
of a man intensely in love and terribly threatened
with the loss of that love. Indeed, if any accusation

of inhumanity were to be brought against Milton
it should be that a man does not often realize so intensely as this poetry declares the effect of such a
threatened loss. Eve, waking on the fatal morning,
has persuaded Adam not to forbid her to work by
herself.[1] And there has followed one of the most
exciting passages of the poem—the thrilling temptation of Eve. Even the temptation of Othello is not
more full of suspense and terror. As it opens with
that humble, solemn, and subtle invocation, the
heart of the reader begins to beat quicker:

> Wonder not, sovran Mistress, if perhaps
> Thou canst, who art sole Wonder;

and thence the plausible reasoning proceeds, much
as Iago's proceeds with Othello. For discursive
reasoning is now directed against intuitive Reason,
and prevails. Illusory perceptions of the individual
self are awakened till they distract attention from
the perception of facts as they are. Reasoning proceeds with both Eve and Othello, as we shall see

---

[1] To this same question of inhumanity two quotations are relevant. When Adam demurs,

> the Virgin Majesty of Eve
> As one who loves and some unkindness meets
> With sweet austere composure thus replied.

Who does not know the 'sweet austere composure' of a woman,
justly (as she thinks), if slightly, offended? And what more exact
words could define it? As one reads one almost shivers under the
chill in Eve's eyes and voice. The second quotation is

> So saying, from her husband's hand her hand
> Soft she withdrew.

The lingering parting of lovers is all there; the sensation of a sensation: the very substance of that soft hand recognized with glory
not its own.

later, precisely as it had done with Satan himself, as
—in a concentrated moment—it had done with
Troilus, to the end of causing its victim to think
himself or herself 'impaired'.

> Why then was this forbid? Why but to awe?
> Why but to keep ye low and ignorant?
> What are gods that man may not become?
>   His forbidding
> Commends thee more, while it infers the good
> By thee communicated, and our want.

And then the climax of that impairment, so supposed to be remedied, arrives, and we feel the
wound no less than Earth:

> So saying, her rash hand [1] in evil hour
> Forth reaching to the fruit, she plucked, she ate.

It is after this that, with mingled motives but with
one motive predominating, she hurries to find
Adam. Her chief motive is still that passion for
him which had filled her but so brief a while before;
and when she meets him, and tells him, there is
revealed in him a corresponding passion.

> So dear I love him, that with him all deaths
> I could endure, without him live no life.

So Eve. And Adam:

> The sacred fruit forbidden! some cursed fraud
> Of enemy hath beguiled thee, yet unknown,

[1] How different from that soft hand which had so sweetly
abandoned that of her lord and her lover but four hundred lines
before! Certainly Milton may have been mistaken in his complete subordination of the woman to the man, but certainly also
that subordination has nowhere been more persuasively breathed.

And me with thee hath ruined, for with thee
Certain my resolution is to die;
How can I live without thee, how forgo
Thy sweet converse and love so dearly joined,
To live again in these wild woods forlorn?
Should God create another Eve, and I
Another rib afford, yet loss of thee
Would never from my heart; no, no, I feel
The link of nature draw me: flesh of flesh,
Bone of my bone thou art, and from thy state
Mine never shall be parted, bliss or woe.

But that is to himself; yet he utters aloud to her
the same resolution, and she leaps to accept it.

However I with thee have fixt my lot,
Certain to undergo like doom, if death
Consort with thee, death is to me as life;
So forcible within my heart I feel
The bond of nature draw me to my own,
My own in thee, for what thou art is mine;
Our state cannot be severed, we are one,
One flesh; to lose thee were to lose my self.

So Adam, and thus Eve to him replied,
O glorious trial of exceeding love,
Illustrious evidence, example high!
Engaging me to emulate, but short
Of thy perfection, how shall I attain,
Adam, from whose dear side I boast me sprung,
And gladly of our Union hear thee speak,
One heart, one soul in both; whereof good proof
This day affords, declaring thee resolved,
Rather than death or aught than death more dread
Shall separate us, linkt in love so dear,
To undergo with me one guilt, one crime.

This is not much below the farthest imagination

of romantic passion : not much below—if it is below—the destiny of Antony and Cleopatra ; the
poetry of Actium itself holds no greater recognition
of devotion and death than the poetry of the Fall.
But in the love of that Egyptian pair, already en-
gulfed and bewildered, there is presented in their
destined fidelity a kind of present redemption ; in
these once Paradisal creatures there can, by the very
nature of the poem, be none. For if the deed were
anything but evil then the state of beatitude which
scores of hundreds of lines had described and intensified would be false. It cannot be ; the whole
imagination of the poem, all the sanctities of heaven,
the beauty of Raphael alighting and the bright
pomp that accompanied Messias, the authority of
Adam and the virgin majesty of Eve herself, sweep
on to the rejection of that devotion, however beautiful it may seem :

> In recompense (for such compliance bad
> Such recompense best merits) from the bough
> She gave him of that fair enticing fruit
> With liberal hand.

In the one word 'bad' Milton recalled the poetic
horror of disobedience, Satan, and hell. But his intelligence did not stop merely at denunciation. It
proceeded to analyse the result ; and the first result
is the immediate change in Adam and Eve. The
change takes place in two ways (i) all that they were
is coarsened, (ii) what each of them was at once each
of them now is sequentially. They had been in-
tended, they had been created, to be in a state of
lordship and service at once, of domination and of
subordination. They were obedient to God and

lords of the world beside. But now, drunk with desire—they can hardly stop eating—they are first triumphant and indulgent, in a coarse imitation of serene mastery, and then gloomy and fearful, in a coarse imitation of serene obedience. Bravado is substituted for honour and fear for holy fear. It is not unfortunately possible for a poet to get Eternity or the schism of eternity into his work. But perhaps this break-up of a congruent harmony of opposites simultaneously existing into a hostile discord of opposites moving in a fatal procession of horror comes as near it as can be imagined. They are 'tost and turbulent', because Reason has been subdued by Appetite, and not until Appetite has been again assumed into Reason, and the two together have regained their power; not, that is to say, until *Paradise Regained*, can that turbulency be finally subdued. It is to be noted that they even boast of the very devotion which—for what it was worth— they had shown to each other ; that also has now become a means of knowing themselves in the con-flicting awareness of good and evil. Not the least accuracy of *Paradise Lost* is that they are given everything that was promised. The fruit was the knowledge of good and evil. But the knowledge of good they already had ; remained but the know-ledge of evil, and that they now have.

Yet, moving as the mortal story is, the narrative of the poem had carried the first sin still farther back into the nature of Satan ; and the nature of Satan had provided another presentation of the same disobedience. But that disobedience of his results in providing what, to be the great complex it is, the

poem needed, but Adam and Eve could not well
supply: it needed an example of a complete and
utter rejection of the Good in terms of mortal imagination. Adam and Eve must have penitence and
room for penitence. But there must also be some
one for whom there was neither; he was found, and
was found to be Satan. Rather, he found himself
when he lit upon Niphates, and examined his mind.
In that speech Milton presented at once Satan and
his own rejection of Satan. The two passions are
closely intertwined, but the second consists in the
presentation of the Divine Nature. In Satan, they
have told us, Milton was at home; Satan is the 'hero'
of *Paradise Lost*; and they are quite right. Satan
is the greatest individual figure of *Paradise Lost*;
he is the author of paradise lost, and therefore,
in a sense, of *Paradise Lost*. And all of Milton's
capacity for heroism and immortal defiance, having
no outlet anywhere else in the poem, because of the
nature of the plot, got itself put into Satan. But
the heroism of immortal defiance is not the only
virtue of humanity, nor did the humanity of Milton
suppose it to be. It is not by making Satan less but
by making the rest of the poem as much more than
Satan as it actually is that we approach an understanding of it. Satan for the first two books was
given a free hand. Certainly his statements require
to be checked a little—not that he is deliberately
deceiving us, but because of a maxim which Milton
very justly put into his mouth, but the corollary
of which perhaps Satan (also quite justly) was not
allowed to perceive, though Milton knew it well
enough. The maxim is—'Better to reign in hell

than serve in heaven'. The corollary is that, in such a case, you will lose the sense of what heaven is like. You will therefore be likely to hold false views of what has actually happened in heaven. Satan, however intelligent, is at the beginning of the poem already falling into this trap. He asserts that he and his angels, in war against God, 'shook his throne'; he asserts that God 'doubted his empire'. This is part of Satan's own magnificent consciousness of things; it is a glorious self-confidence, and in that great verse it convinces us. But farther on in the poem, in verse serener and happier, and more ironic, than Satan's, we discover that it is not true. God

> Smiling to his only Son thus said . . .
> Nearly it now concerns us to be sure
> Of our omnipotence . . .
>   lest unawares we lose
> This our high place, our sanctuary, our hill.
> To whom the Son, with calm aspect and clear
> Lightening divine, ineffable, serene,
> Made answer:—'Mighty Father, thou thy foes
> Justly hast in derision.'

It is again the intermingling of the narrative retreat and the psychological advance; the Divine utterance had chronological priority, but the ironic fact is the poetic sequence of Satan's obstinacy. The fact is that when Milton said 'Omnipotent' he meant Omnipotent. He never imagined God could be disturbed; but he imagined that Satan might think he was, Satan having lost all sense of proportion. Milton is often accused of not having had any sense of humour, and indeed *Paradise Lost* does rather

maintain a stately seriousness. But the notion that
any created being could overthrow the uncreated
seems to have appeared to him as gently amusing.
It was perhaps with a similar amusement that he
allowed Satan (having refused the angelic perception which Raphael defined) to be led into the false
belief that Reason would equal God with the angels.

> Fardest from him is best
> Whom reason hath equalled, force hath made supreme
> Above his equals. Farewell, happy fields,
> Where joy for ever dwells : Hail, horrors, hail,
> Infernal world, and thou, profoundest hell,
> Receive thy new possessor : one who brings
> A mind not to be changed by place or time.
> The mind is its own place, and in itself
> Can make a heaven of hell, and hell of heaven.

Nothing can diminish the superb heroism, the arch-
angelic greatness of *that*. But at the same time nothing
can alter the fact that it is by no means as true as
Satan thinks it is.

The supreme absurdity, hopelessness, and sinful-
ness of Satan's attitude is summed up in a line, but the
line is postponed for a little. There is the council
of Pandemonium, the departure of Satan, the terrific
journey through Chaos, all which incidents increase
the heroism and determination of his sublime figure.
But it is not merely for Satan's own sake that so
much rich poetry is spent on him; it is for the
poem's and for the imagination of a greater sublimity.
Milton did everything he could to make the fallen
archangel effective, and having created him Milton's
imagination refused him. The great and the only
quarrel among readers of Milton is over the question:

Did his intellect or his imagination reject Satan? Every reader must settle it for himself. The present writer has no doubt that it was his imagination and that *Paradise Lost* conveys that imagination. It even does it in a line, though it amplifies that line. The line is

> Warring in heaven against heaven's matchless king.

One can but speak personally in these matters : I find that line as wonderful and as final as anything in Milton. A supreme serenity is in it, though Satan speaks it ; and its serenity is the measure of Satan's own futility and despair. How hopeless, how *silly* to war in heaven against heaven's matchless king ! Yes, but the line is more; it is the definition of man's continual effort and therefore of his continual sin and failure. In a sweep of seven words Milton defined man's continual strife with his perception of Beauty, defined and despised, reproved and rejected it. But he knew all about it. Or would have done, had he been less inhuman.

Let it be supposed that he did; that this soliloquy, the soliloquy of absolute despair, is in fact a document only inhuman in the sense that Lear's soliloquies are inhuman, because it and they are the definitions by great imaginations of states greatly beyond our normal being. Despair then is analysing itself in approaching its climax. It hates the sun because the sun is a symbol of the state against which pride and worse ambition rebelled, warring in heaven against heaven's matchless king. But what is this heaven? It is a state where the exquisite paradox of human love at its finest is true of

the very nature of life itself; where what we know
but for a moment or two is the very definition of
existence. It is the state in which the blessed recognition of generous love is at once the complete
corresponding reply to that love :

> a grateful mind
> By owing owes not but still pays, at once
> Indebted and discharged.

The grateful mind would not lose the debt it has
already discharged; the debt is the means of its
gratitude, and its gratitude is the deliverance of
its soul, its very way of life, and the activity of its
creation. Against such a deliverance, such a putting-
forth of himself in subordinate joy, Satan rebels.
Afterwards he is shown in revolt against the appearance of the Divine Word (who is itself the complete
embodiment of the gratitude that Satan rejects). But
that is the psychological localizing of his nature.
The greater precedes the less; in the beginning he
is opposed to the whole character of heaven, not to
its manifestations. He objects to having anything
given him; he objects to the nature of love. And
he objects to it for another reason: he hates 'heaven's
free love dealt equally to all'. It would not do to
compare too closely this objection with Troilus's
complaint against Cressida; there is a moral possibility in one which is not in the other. But when
and if the most extreme moral objection to Cressida's
action has been allowed, when her natural selfishness
has been admitted, still it is true that Troilus's actual
suffering arises not from moral disapproval but from
personal disappointment. Cressida's free love is certainly much more like our own general interpretation

of those words than is the free love of heaven. But Troilus's imposition of fidelity is as far from the gratitude of heaven as is Satan's. One cannot be full of happy gratitude if one is always saying, 'Be true; put me first'. Even if the primacy exists such a clamant realization of it is improper. 'Put me first', say Troilus and Satan and Othello and Lear. That is not to identify the other partners in the respective colloquies.

But Satan does not stop there; he goes on to hate the free love itself because it follows its own nature and not his. He has rebelled, in the name of freedom, against the central nature of freedom. He is to be free but God is not to be free, because if God is free heaven will be heaven. And it is precisely heaven being heaven to which Satan so violently objects. Recognizing (one might say) the force of his objection, heaven obligingly, so far as he is concerned, turns itself into hell. And the soliloquy proceeds to call up in us a knowledge of our capacities for rejecting what we know as good and beautiful and refuse to enjoy as good and beautiful. There is no way out of that refusal except by submission to the apprehended goodness and beauty of love giving itself freely:

> the thousand acts that Deity supreme
> Doth ease its heart of love in.

Why will not a man do this? Because he would despise himself; he would not be a man if he submitted; he will stand upon his rights. There is but one objection to standing on your rights; it is that the pronoun cancels the noun, and there are none. Satan has invented his rights, it is true. He considers

abandoning them; what if he *could* repent? It is an
intellectual hypothesis; he does not mean to, because
he believes hate has taken the place of love.

> . . . never can true reconcilement grow,
> Where wounds of deadly hate have pierced so deep.

He can never be reconciled to Love, because he
hates Love. He cannot hope; he will not fear.
There can then be no change but to plunge from
agony to agony, in despair which is complete hell
and yet opens on deeper hells: '*all* good to me is
lost'. All that can be done is to go on madly warring
with heaven's matchless king; perhaps somebody
can be hurt somewhere. There have been a number
of people who have felt like that; what but their
emotions fill our prisons and law-courts? our streets
and houses? our gardens and drawing-rooms? What
but our knowledge of our pain and hate and despair
recognizes itself in the pitiless imagination of Milton?
He was in that sense inhuman; he saw and revealed
to men the pit of darkness into which, in their souls,
they cast their souls; by that at least

> Divided Empire with heaven's King I hold.

We shall never begin to apprehend Milton unless
we understand that when he said 'heaven' he really
meant something like 'heaven'—a place of joyous
interchange of free and willing love. There is in
Satan a growing incapacity to understand what the
word 'love' means. He sees Adam and Eve, and he
reflects that he is sorry for them—

> whom my thoughts pursue
> With pity and could love, so lively shines
> In them divine resemblance. . .

only he will gather them into hell. It is only his
own magnificent serious belief in himself that makes
that speech convincing ; it would otherwise be too
like the *Walrus and the Carpenter*. But in effect it
is a magnificent passage because Satan is perfectly
serious ; he believes he could love were it not for
necessity. And what then by now did Satan think
that love was ? It is perhaps relevant to note that
the Power from which all the sanctities of heaven
drew 'beatitude past utterance' knew nothing of
necessity : 'what I will is Fate' ; and that Raphael
knew nothing either—'freely we serve Because we
freely love'. All opposition—violent or evasive—
to that experience Milton splendidly imagined; all
opposition to that understanding he oversoared. It is
in his dispersal of those mists that the glory of *Paradise Lost* lies; the poetic glory which embodied forms
and substances—of rebellion, of greed, and of the
upright heart and pure, and of the Spirit and Power
which inform it.

(iv) But what then is this Power against which
Satan rebels, and the definition of which is at the
same time, by contraries, a definition of Satan ? It
is (if one may say so) Milton's poor unfortunate
God and the relations of created beings with that
God.

The God of *Paradise Lost* (let it be said again)
does not exist outside *Paradise Lost* any more than
Macbeth exists outside *Macbeth*. No doubt it is a
pleasant game to discuss how far, if at all, Macbeth had conceived the murder of Duncan before he
appears in the play striding forward under a sky of
mingled foulness and fairness on the road to Forres.

But before then Macbeth never existed. It is an
equally pleasant game to discuss which of the innumerable Trinitarian heresies Milton had fallen into,
and how far the poem compels us to regard it as
Arian, and once we have got away from the poem
we may enjoy ourselves for hours discussing it, with
the *Encyclopaedia* and several histories of Christian
doctrine to keep us informed. But to do that we
must get away from the poem, as we must get away
from the *Prelude* to discuss Wordsworth's relations
with Annette, or from the *Ring and the Book* to discuss whether Pompilia was indeed all that she should
have been, or Innocent IX the Papal wisdom whose
voice informs the November evening. The God of
Paradise Lost must be taken at the valuation the
poem puts on him ; we may or may not like him
morally, but poetically we have no other way even
of disliking him. Nobody, I suppose, seriously believes in that distressed God of some of Hardy's
poems, who had got himself hopelessly involved in
his own unceasing creation, but for the sake of the
poems we accept him in the poems. The only evidence we have about the God of the *Paradise* is the
evidence of *Paradise Lost* and *Paradise Lost* has no
doubt on the matter.

> About him all the sanctities of heaven
> Stood thick as stars, and from his sight received
> Beatitude past utterance.

> To whom the Son, with calm aspect, and clear
> Lightening divine, ineffable, serene.

> O Father, O Supreme of heavenly Thrones,
> First, Highest, Holiest, Best.

Joy and love,
Uninterrupted joy, unrivalled love.

This is the fundamental beauty of existence. (It is such a pity that Milton never understood what joy and love were like.) But the poem involves joy and love in an unwavering recognition of facts; that is, by the perception of Reason in its most exalted mood. Its recognition is proved by the Niphates analysis.

Whatever the *Ode to a Nightingale* was to do, *Paradise Lost* approaching in its own way a universe dissimilar in its poetic habit but not so dissimilar in its poetic recognition of intense life, refused to leave the intellect behind. The dull brain was not to be abandoned; on the contrary it was to be irradiated and then trusted. Reason (the great arch-angel asserted) is the soul's being, 'discursive or intuitive'. Man would have been created futilely (the Almighty proclaims) were he without 'Will, and Reason (Reason also is choice)'. In the soul (Adam explains to Eve, awaking from her dream of harm) 'Are many lesser faculties that serve Reason as chief' and proceeds to a discussion of the dominance of the irrational subconsciousness during sleep.

Reason then is the chief faculty of the soul, and Reason is choice; Reason also may be discursive or intuitive, the latter chiefly along angels, the former chiefly among men. The intellect is capable of clear and certain knowledge; among angels this knowledge is more of the nature of vision—that is, of simultaneous perception, among men of logic—that is, of harmonious sequential perception; though neither entirely excludes the other. They are the same in kind; they differ but in degree. Learned

men have taught us from what sources the genius
of Milton drew its distinctions on this point. From
whatever source they came, their effect here is now
the important thing. The intellect beholds, either
in a flash or sequentially, its choice between obedience and disobedience; its law is Reason. In
obedience to this Reason lies its own happiness,
which its being naturally desires. In this sense it
recognizes beauty to be truth and truth to be beauty.
Were it otherwise, were it predestined to obey,
there could be no choice, therefore no active exercise
of the will fulfilling its choice, therefore no interchange of joy.

> Freely we serve
> Because we freely love; as in our will
> To love or not; in this we stand or fall.

But love is a matter of the intellect and the will;
sensation of beatitude is (at least in man's unfallen
state: it seems somehow to be different now) a result
of this.

That mortal joy at any rate reposes in such a
manner in the exercise of interchanged wills is a fact
of experience. It is this fact of experience upon
which (one might almost say) *Paradise Lost* is sensationally based. The delighted interchange of devotion between Adam and Eve is the mirror (in the
poem) and perhaps some such experience is the
actual source (out of the poem) of his exaltation of
choice. Milton was, of course, inhuman, so we could
not expect him to realize the highest delights of
mortal love. Had he realized them, had his imagination been capable of so transcending ours as to shape

a vision of intense 'complacency' (to use a technical term) then *Paradise Lost* would have thrilled to an intense centre. Then we, following that lofty song, might have begun to realize how far beyond our senses the mere sound of the verses echoes.

It is true that the poem has its theological side, and it may even be admitted that sometimes its theological side almost interferes with its poetic. Sometimes when the Perfect Good is uttering its opinion of itself one feels for a moment that it is more perfect than good. God perhaps ought not to be quite so conscious of his own deity : a little modesty would be gratifying. One would be glad to hear him occasionally explaining to the angels that it is no credit to him that he is God. Presumably if you are uncreated, you can hardly claim any merit for it. Even Christianity has never authoritatively formulated a decision on the question how far God must be held responsible for his own existence, presumably because he enjoys it and it is doubtful how far his creatures have a moral right to demand the self-annihilation of an existence whose chief drawback is that it seems to involve their existence also. Besides, he is said to have meant us to enjoy both our own and his, and the same Christianity has even declared that he fully accepted—by the Word in deed —responsibility for our present lack of enjoyment. However that may be, the God of *Paradise Lost* is sometimes a little portentous and self-attentive ; it is the natural difficulty of continuing to be sublime, which has been occasionally remarked to exist in the whole poem as in one of its chief personages. But God has less opportunity of modulation even

than the poem ; he cannot become Satan or Adam
or Eve for a change. There is in him no variableness nor shadow of turning ; so he goes on repeating
himself on his high place, his sanctuary, his hill.
Unless the angels are singing a choric ode, when
presumably he reposes in gratified attention, or unless he pauses to send one of them on a quite
unnecessary errand merely 'to ensure Our prompt
obedience'.

It is a fantastic picture—God sending an angel
on an errand merely to be sure that he does it, and
it is made even more fantastic by our continual
imposition of our own notions of what God is like
upon the God of *Paradise Lost*. But it must be
admitted that Milton is struggling with a problem
which even his genius could hardly solve. He had to
express Omnipotence and Omniscience ; he had to
set that of which they were qualities into relation
with created beings; and he had to turn the whole
thing into a dramatic narrative. It is very difficult
to put Omnipotence and Omniscience into a story,
because the proportions of the story are immediately
destroyed. In another sense than Cleopatra's, 'the
odds is gone'. It is still more difficult to make them
dramatic; which is why, if Christianity were not true,
it would have been necessary, for the sake of letters,
to invent it. It is the only safe means by which poetry
can compose the heavens, without leaving earth
entirely out of the picture. The Incarnation, had it
not been necessary to man's redemption, would have
been necessary to his art ; the rituals of the Church
have omitted that important fact from their paeans.
Even with the Incarnation Milton tended towards

sublimity; the comparison of his ode with Crashaw's shows the difference between a ceremonious and a tender adoration. The sense of adoration is awakened by both poems, but the bright-harnessed angels could never have been so sweetly rebuked by mortals for the coldness of their fleeces ; nor could those other challenged cherubs have made so lofty a guard for the infant victor over Osiris and Pan. And when Milton's genius had risen from the earth to contemplate the essential being of Godhead, and to behold that in a poem, he seems to be moving beyond even the highest reaches of a human wit, and human wit sees his error. Yet the poem had to have its God, and its God had to be omnipotent, omniscient, and omni-benevolent. In the narrative poem God is a very important character, as he had to be, and the details are sometimes unconvincing : not quite as unconvincing as they are apt to be if we introduce this and that notion borrowed from St. Thomas or Wesley or the Book of Common Prayer, but still unconvincing. But in the psychological poem things are easier ; for there the part of God is but a personification of something else. He—as best he can —personifies the mystery of heaven.

Heaven (to recall the phrases of our childhood) is not a place but a state. Heaven in *Paradise Lost* is a place but it is also a state. It is a state of which the holy and invoked light is the first-born, the light which irradiates the mind and reveals things invisible. It is the state in which all that exists is open to the view of the Spirit and the delight of and in the Spirit, in which Satan raised impious war, and from which he was, as a natural necessity, cast out.

It is a state which expels all rebels, persons or
emotions, and always rejoicing, closes itself perfectly
against their rage ; a state in which sanctities appear
thick as stars ; of which the properties and nature
must be reckoned by things on earth and are perhaps more like them than is thought ; which indeed
will, by men's long obedience, come at last to be
one with earth. It is a state to which throughout
the poem, all beauty and joy is continually referred,
till its name becomes an ideograph for beauty and
joy ; but also a state which has its own fixed laws
perceived by Reason and necessary to be obeyed
by all who desire still to be inhabited by it as a state
of being, just as in the narrative they inhabit it as
a place of being. In that narrative God is the creator
of heaven ; but psychologically he is rather, as it
were, its climax—heaven utterly experiencing itself
and freed from the knowledge of any dependence
or possibility of alteration. And therefore this side
is best reflected again into the narrative by the
Divine Son rather than by the Paternal Deity on
whom, as a narrative, it necessarily depends. It is
the Divine Son who is either way the hinge of the
poem, for on the one hand it is on their first knowledge of him that the angels of disobedience rebel ;
on the other, it is by contrast with his obedience that
the other disobediences are known. He, in a double
sense, manifests as heaven ; he is heaven in its approach to and apprehension of its perfect climax,
and also he is heaven in its relation to all rebellious,
erring, and even exterior powers. But there are but
two exterior powers—one is hell, and that is rather
erected by Satan than by heaven ('which way I fly

is hell; myself am hell'), and one is Chaos. Chaos
certainly is rather arbitrarily invented by the poem,
unless we are willing to accept its own suggestion
that God leaves Chaos chaotic merely because he so
chooses. It exists because he fills infinitude; it is
chaotic because he does not put forth his goodness
over it. It does not, after all, hurt any one—not even
itself. Over Chaos he merely extends his empire.[1] But
over the rebel angels he extends his strength, because
they have elected to compare their strength—

> since by strength
> They measure all, of other excellence
> Not emulous, nor care who them excels,
> Nor other strife with them do I vouchsafe.

But we have discussed the expulsion from heaven
earlier; it is one of Milton's more human moments,
and practically every one can recognize it on looking into the more unpleasant moments of his past
life. The only reason why it is not immediately

---

[1] It would be falsely ingenious to see any comparison of value
in the fact that Satan beholds Chaos himself while the Son does
not. But it is, I hope, not ingenious to remark the difference
between the superb poetic effect of the difficult journey of Satan
through the abyss, and the equally superb poetic effort of the sub-
ordinating progress through it of the Word.

> Silence, ye troubled waves, and thou Deep, peace,
> Said then the Omnific Word, your discord end:
>   Nor stayed, but on the wings of cherubim
> Uplifted, in paternal glory rode
> Far into Chaos, and the world unborn;
> For Chaos heard his voice: him all his train
> Followed in bright procession to behold
> Creation, and the wonders of his might.

It is not so heroic. But it is Power and Beauty in serene
operation.

recognized is that we are all of us living in hell
to such an extent that it seems unfair for us not to
be masters of and in heaven. But that is a moral
decision about the nature of obedience and heaven,
and not a poetic. In poetry according to Milton that
is what happens when pride and worse ambition
war in heaven against heaven's matchless king.

In effect, it is those two words, *obedience* and
heaven, which carry the poem; Reason understands
them in the poem, and perhaps has something to do
with understanding the poem by them. Heaven is
defined, directly or indirectly, in passage after great
passage, as a state of Power and Reason and Beauty.
It is personified into Deity, and the angels, and
Adam and Eve. God is its climax, and also its
definition as 'unbegotten'; heaven simply exists.
'Heaven's free love dealt equally to all' is a recognized truth of existence, whether we like or dislike
it. It is a state in which man exists by willingly and
joyously recognizing facts—natural facts and moral
facts—as far as he can. The poem imagines man
(as man) in a state of complete spiritual freedom,
and therefore as able to recognize quite simply
and beautifully as we in our fallen—or, at least, in
our present—state cannot. But there will be facts
which rightly compel submission as there will be facts
which rightly demand lordship. The implication
is that in a state of high and passionate morality—
of heaven—you will know which facts are which.
But it is possible so to indulge a state of pride,
ambition, and selfish lusts, that the Reason which
declares this to the soul is obscured and lost; and
with Reason go Power and Beauty. The self-loving

spirit loses these things as the self-abandoning spirit discovers them. Self-love exists in Satan, and is pursued to the most extreme point of its quite inevitable despair. Self-love also exists in Adam and Eve, and it is mingled with perverse follies of sinful devotion. But self-abandonment also exists in them, and the complexity of the poem unites that to the heavenly self-abandonment of Christ.

At the extreme end of *Paradise Lost* the lowest in the hierarchy of rationally percipient creatures, looking to her immediate lord, recognizes with a passion of realism her abandonment to him, to obedience, and to her future motherhood of the heaven of reconciliation.

> Whence thou return'st and whither went'st I know;
> For God is also in sleep, and dreams advise,
> Which he hath sent propitious, some great good
> Presaging, since, with sorrow and heart's distress
> Wearied, I fell asleep: but now lead on;
> In me is no delay; with thee to go
> Is to stay here; without thee here to stay
> Is to go hence unwilling; thou to me
> Art all things under heaven, all places thou,
> Who for my wilful crime art banished hence.
> This further consolation yet secure
> I carry hence: though all by me is lost,
> Such favour I unworthy am vouchsafed,
> By me the Promised Seed shall all restore.

The 'Promised Seed' is the Divine Son of the poem; it is that mirror of entire beauty which here the mirror of the poetry reflects. Heaven's glory climbs above Eve to its climax in God, in its own state of unbegotten Reason and Power and Beauty,

and that climax involves the imagination of its own
entire submission to itself. The full deific initiative
of heaven Milton could hardly present; heaven for
him had to know itself perfectly to some point short
of that. It must then willingly abandon itself only
to find that it realizes itself utterly so. *Paradise Lost*
is a poem of its own kind, with great heroic personages, neither quite Christian (in the narrative
sense) nor quite Pagan; with Gods upon whom we
may comment and arguments with which we may
disagree, as we may with the persons and ideas of
Shakespeare's plays. It has a created mythology
of its own, which we have to accept as its own.
Day and Night repose alternately in a cave of
the heavenly sanctuary, a chariot rushes out of the
armoury of God to sustain the Divine Son, the
rebel angels invent artillery, the Son who is co-
eternal is begotten in time, and so on; we can
all add to the list of local materializations which we
may find it difficult to accept. But the materializa-
tion is a necessity of the poem, and we have to accept
it because otherwise we cannot have the poem. Accepted, it gives us all its own tremendous greatness.
But that greatness is shot through and through with
the other greatness of states of being profoundly
imagined in relation to the one main theme of
obedience and disobedience. This perhaps even
more than Milton's views of the relation of the
sexes is the poetic cause of Eve's submission to
Adam; he spoke of the exterior general principle
too often, but the incarnation of it is one with the
whole great harmony. We must yield ourselves
even to that while we read, if we want to read the

poem, unpoetically consoling ourselves with the reflection that people in love do have all sorts of quaint ideas. The fallen Eve saw the absurdity of it—which also is part of the poem. But unfallen or repentant she accepted the necessity which the theme of the poem laid on her; she consented to be one with that intervolved obedience; and, consenting, recovered her place and her passion. Her passion answers at a distance the passion of the Divine Son—

> thou to me
> Art all things under heaven, all places thou;
> this I my glory account,
> My exaltation, and my whole delight,
> That thou in me well pleased declar'st thy will
> Fulfilled, which to fulfil is all my bliss.

This is what it is not to war in heaven against heaven's matchless king; and heaven's matchless king is not only the God of the poem, but the whole state of percipient delight defined by the poem. Once, for a moment, even Satan—at the sight of Eve—lost himself.

> That space the Evil One abstracted stood
> From his own evil, and for the time remained
> Stupidly good.

It was, by then, his only possibility of goodness; the word 'stupidly' is the opposite of the intelligential joy of Raphael. Against that stupid goodness there exists the creative goodness of the Son, the 'Promised Seed'. Those words there are not merely Christian; they are poetic. The entire power of the self-abandoning spirit is to be Eve's child; reason is

to be born in her. At one remove Michael declares
the same high promise to Adam.

> Then wilt thou not be loth
> To leave this Paradise, but shalt possess
> A Paradise within thee, happier far.
> Let us descend now therefore from this top
> Of speculation.

It was the paradise of a heart and mind self-
abandoned in a lovely subordination to an accepted good which Milton beheld from his top of
speculation ; he saw the nature of man such that it
had to discover that mystery. The kindred mutations by which he transmuted the world into the
great Nature which exists in his own mighty poetry
may be philosophically wrong. But his imagination
beheld sanctities—and realistic sanctities—thick as
stars; it is a description of *Paradise Lost* itself. The
whole complex poem, yielding fresh poetic truth
every time it is opened, contains those sanctities,
as it contains Satan, in the power and reason and
beauty of its style.

It is why Keats found it 'a greater wonder every
day'; it is why the close describes not only Adam
and Eve leaving Paradise, but ourselves finding
ourselves exiled from the paradise of intelligent
love. The poem has contained its own great nature,
the highest reaches of the human wit, the top of
speculation from which are seen the nature of
humanity with its awareness of perfect experience,
its knowledge of the duties and joys native to such
experience, and of the varying possibilities of its
own action. Heaven and hell define each other, but
heaven can exist without hell and hell cannot exist

without heaven since heaven's free love is its hell.
The journeys in which the poem is so rich—Satan's,
Abdiel's, Raphael's, Christ's, Adam's—again define
the relation of spiritual heaven and spiritual hell to
all existing things. The final departure is in ourselves; but it is also a definition of our parting from
Paradise Lost. Our subordinated minds, having had
to turn to an actual world less powerful, less lovely,
less rational, look back, remembering how they
themselves, leaving behind them the flaming cheru-
bim, the happy seat, the Messias of its Miltonic
imagination—how they also, closing the book,

> with lingering steps and slow
> Through Eden took their solitary way.

IX

THE ABOLITION OF SIGNIFICANCE

Such then was the august power of imagination that answered the half-unreal maxim of Keats and searched out one aspect of the only half-understood anguish of Troilus; that raised the allegory of Spenser to a place of identities and justified beyond any other English poetic effort the pathetic philosophy of Pope; that, finally, exemplified in an even more sovereign passion than his own the clearest insight of Wordsworth into the nature of poetry. The conflict of which these had all, in their degree, been aware is here subordinated to a pervading and intuitive Reason, which is also Power and Beauty. And the harmony is that of a moral composure, expressed not so much in terms of theological dogma as of the very nature of man. But even Milton could not experience both methods of exploration at once; could not, from his Snowdon (let us say—his Tabor), behold two opposite visions at once. This is man in Reason. But what of man without Reason? He left that to Shakespeare.[1]

'If beauty have a soul this is not she.' 'Beauty has a soul', Milton, in effect, answers, 'and this is she. Listen.' And, God helping us, we do. But Shakespeare on the contrary answered, 'Beauty has no soul; neither is this she. Let us see what we can do on that hypothesis.

O madness of discourse,
That cause sets up with and against itself.

[1] It is true Shakespeare had already done it. But Milton would have left it anyhow.

S

Let us have a little more madness of discourse, and see where it leads.' It is, after all, not an unsuitable preliminary meditation to *Othello, Lear,* and *Macbeth.* But there is an important new element in the procedure.

Wordsworth had sung ('like a lark'—the *Prelude!*) of sublimity. Milton had, so to speak, taken him at his word and produced an even greater effect of sublime glory. He had defined what, as well as how, all souls feel; he had revealed forms and substances in glory not their own; his genius had felt the voices of the abyss issuing forth to silent light in one continuous stream. But sublimity is not the only method which poetry can take to express itself; or rather, even sublimity may occasionally choose to laugh, although it may then have to permit itself to change a little in the process. Wordsworth cannot be said to have laughed. Milton—even of Milton we cannot say more than that a faint smile crosses his face whenever he contemplates the ironic efforts of impotence to attack Omnipotence, and the hope of Satan that he will destroy, of Adam that he will evade, the process of the immitigable beauty of the laws of heaven. He smiles with subdued amusement, and then the smile is stopped

> upon the wing by sound
> Of harmony from Heaven's remotest spheres,

and he turns in a purer and graver contemplation to see the Archangel alighting 'like Maia's son', or the Divine Word serenely proceeding through Chaos. In such company, Milton with them and we with Milton, one does not laugh. It is a sublime gravity, but it is gravity.[1]

But Shakespeare refused to allow gravity to have it all its own way. There is laughter in *Troilus*; there is a frank smile in *Othello*; there is at least the feel of a smile in *Lear*; and these smiles and laughters are not ironic or moral; they are at things, simply things as at that moment seen. Perhaps the only play of Shakespeare's where there is neither a smile nor opportunity for a smile is *Macbeth*; and reason good, if indeed *Macbeth* is a poetic imagination of the earth feeding on itself.

It is proper that we should not be on the track of sublimity here, for we are not following the Reason which sees into the life of things. It may follow us, if it will; that is, it may follow Shakespeare. That it can do as it likes about. But what Shakespeare is doing from *Hamlet* onwards is twofold: he is exploring the actual schism in reason, and pressing it as much farther as he can. The perception of man is hereafter to be horribly doubled. He was interested enough in the *Troilus* kind of catastrophe to repeat it in *Othello*, having found the poetic—and almost metaphysical—formula for it. In *Lear* he changed the catastrophe; he almost introduced another character, a silent and invisible part, a goddess spoken of and invoked or defied,

[1] There is, of course, the elephant. It was no doubt Adam and Eve's unfallen state of innocence which enabled them to be amused at the elephant's efforts. He seems to us to have so little scope for entertainment; one would think he would have to repeat his effects so often. But there again—in an unfallen state boredom at repetition would not exist.

NB Nature a person, a goddess among the subtextual dramatis personae

Natura Rerum, the nature of things. In *Macbeth* he proceeded to the full operation of falsehood, still summoning *Natura Rerum* to provide 'the odds' in the background. If he had gone on still the same way after *Macbeth*, it is difficult to imagine what might have happened; fortunately, he did not. He became interested in *Natura Rerum* itself; *Antony* is approaching that state—things as they are. The characters of the last comedies defined it.

Othello provides the same plot as *Troilus*, plus Iago. And Iago is the introduction of a new element into the matter, an element which looks in one sense like an avoiding of the problem but in another like an accentuation of it. For (i) his argument is false, and Desdemona is not in love with Cassio; Beauty therefore has actually, so far as Othello is concerned, kept her soul. But (ii) the deliberate erection of Iago is the creation of a rejection of beauty, and of an indifference to the identity of things—to truth. He is Shakespeare's genius at its height, including a 'conceit', a wonder, of the deliberate destruction of beauty. It is a more complex human situation than *Troilus*, but the metaphysical elements are separated and more exactly defined; it is therefore simplified. The symbols are so intensely themselves that they are enabled to be symbols: stability and innocence and destructiveness are defined as philosophical elements by the force of their mortal exactness. It is the great gift of poetry. It is also the cause of one great danger in poetry. By a kind of verbal shorthand we say that Desdemona is this or Othello is that, and forget that neither Desdemona nor Othello nor any other character is anything but Shakespeare's language. That language compressed metaphysics as it compressed humanity, and mingled them with such power that we seem to be in the presence of the necessities of the earth. In *Othello* he approached this absolute power, but in *Lear* he published it, and afterwards he never went back. Tragedy or comedy, he wrote afterwards in that perpetual publication of a universe according to its law—the law of his own style—and that universe with its law is what we have come to mean by Shakespeare. There are moments when we sit up and distrust it—healthy moments when we tend to say 'Look here, what is all this fuss about Shakespeare?' and wonder if we spent the same amount of energy on Mrs. Hemans or Sir Richard Blackmore whether we should not find as much in them. Perhaps we should; the difficulty is that one cannot spend energy on Mrs. Hemans or Blackmore or their like: their poems crumble under it. They cannot sustain our attack. But the absolute power of Shakespeare or Milton still exceeds our own meditations.

It is in the approach to this complete universe that the chance of the Muse provided a phrase which opens on our minds in exactly the opposite direction to the opening of the *Nightingale*.

> My heart aches; and a drowsy numbness pains
>   My sense, as though of hemlock I had drunk,
> Or emptied some dull opiate to the drains
>   A moment since, and Lethewards had sunk.

The drowsy numbness had in *Hamlet* been of another kind, and had sent its victim to another death than that which was imagined beneath the

Nightingale. But the lines are more definitely rejected in *Othello*.

> Not poppy nor mandragora
> Nor all the drowsy syrups of the world
> Shall ever medicine thee to that sweet sleep
> Which thou ow'dst yesterday.

Neither hemlock nor poppy can quench this awareness. It is the definition of Othello, but also of the present poetry. Poetry is no more to be a drowsy syrup, not even with divine drowsiness and the rich sepulchre and the high requiem of the Nightingale; it is to avoid sweet sleep. The night of Desdemona's death and of Lear's madness have no sleep, and the owl and the crickets in the all-but-sleeping castle of Inverness do but accentuate the central wakefulness of murder. Those vigils lie before poetry now. We are not to fade away from the terrors; the dull brain forces us on to their full expression.

Yet the cause of those experiences dwindles, from *Hamlet* to *Lear*. It is as if Shakespeare's genius, little by little, reduced the cause as he intensified the result. When he began the tragedies with *Hamlet*, he used fratricide and regicide to shake the sweet prince's soul. But in *Troilus* he lessened murder to unfaithfulness. No doubt alteration in the beloved is a cause of as much agony as murder can be, but it can hardly be called so unusual or therefore so terrible. And in *Othello* it is not even alteration; it is only supposed alteration. Yet, less as the cause grows, the agony grows more; poetry awakens the sense of a more direct spectacle of change there than it had done in *Hamlet*, where it is rather memory

that is tormented. In *Lear* there is even less actual
cause; the fact—as distinguished from the persons
—of the tragedy is but Cordelia's 'tardiness of
nature'. That the spiritual evil grows more intense
is another matter. Claudius and Cressida are not
such dark powers as Iago, and it might be held that
even Iago is not so simply dreadful as Goneril and
Regan—and had excuse, or what seemed to him
excuse, more proportionable to his acts than Goneril
and Regan to theirs. Certainly the catastrophes
swell in proportion to those powers of destruction.
But the facts that first gave rise to the catastrophes
diminish. Murder, unfaithfulness, supposed unfaithfulness, a tardiness in nature. Even if the fact
of *Othello* is taken to be Iago's lie, it is still but a
hinted untruth. Murder, untruth, hinted untruth,
natural tardiness: so we descend. Contemplated so,
it is as if Shakespeare found himself needing less
and less violence to begin terror. The terror is in
the course of things: 'something may be done that
we will not'. It is. Only when we come to *Macbeth*,
and deliberate choice (as we shall see) accepts a false
identity, is the will of mortals brought again into
question. One might almost think that Shakespeare
abandoned the poetic expression of the will in
choice when he left Angelo to silence in *Measure for
Measure*.

In *Othello* there is no actual fact of changed identity as there had been in *Troilus*, imposed upon the
senses. Beauty has not lost her soul before Othello's
eyes, but he must be persuaded that she has. It
is done by a process of discursive reasoning, that
is, by a continual awakening of perception after

perception, until a final violence of perception beholds the pattern of argument transformed to a living fact. Something like this is involved in all conversion, and Othello is converted. Each painful awakening of each new perception, so perfectly harmonious with what has preceded, adds another touch to Desdemona's new, though it does not destroy her foregone, identity, until at last the fresh and perfect image exists in his mind as clearly as a similar image existed in the mind of Troilus from his attest of eyes and ears. There is, as there was then, still a credence and an obstinate esperance in the heart, but, though it is obstinately strong, it is not strong enough to destroy its rival. One might almost believe that Shakespeare, having done the thing directly in *Troilus*, determined to do it indirectly in *Othello*, as if contemptuous of the visible falsity, and preferring afterwards to give his genius work by offering it an indirect and unreal falsity to make convincing. It is, even so, not Iago who convinces us of himself so much as Othello who convinces us of Iago: always excepting the great mandragora achievement, which consummates the process for us. It is there indeed only for us; Othello does not hear it, and Iago does not need it; it is we who hear, need, and are convinced by it. Yet, though the whole exquisite workmanship of Iago is, as a matter of fact, a sensational craft, it pretends to be rational. He generalizes; he recalls himself to generalization; and when he is not generalizing he is talking about himself. But all the while the delicate shocks are delivered. Men are not what they seem; Cassio may be; Iago himself possesses himself honestly; the jealous man does not; let Othello take care not to be jealous—not to be so divided, till Othello in the very energy of his assertion of his single heart opens his heart to division, and then the division, by examples of Desdemona's past and possible untruths, establishes itself. Yet the generalizations are often true enough; it is in Othello's local application of them that Iago's success and his own error lie, and the spectre of a lascivious Desdemona introduces chaos.

And as the poetry had concerned itself with the presentation of the overthrow of a more mature and less suspicious—a more self-possessed—heart than Troilus had, so it consistently presents a greater overthrow. The violent shock had left the Trojan still in possession of his power, his activity, and his habits ; it had, in fact, increased them. Skirting madness but untaken by it, Troilus doubles his courage and his ferocity; he blames Hector for being too pitiful. But the Moor loses his habitual activity —'Othello's occupation's gone.' Troilus wished to destroy Diomed, but Othello has to root up the whole complex growth which symbolizes to him his impairment and his shame. For Troilus was concerned with the single devastating fact of Cressida's change, but Othello is concerned as greatly with his own knowledge of it. Troilus (to be fair to him) did not identify himself with justice ; only Cressida with injustice. But Othello is driven to this farther identification as his only refuge. It was not (he said) his physical appetites, his 'young affects', that desired Desdemona, nor is it they (he says) that will destroy her. It is decency, honour, righteousness. At least,

Iago never pretended *that*. But it is not decency, only destruction, that Othello craves. He never thinks of Cassio as a rival, only as a villain ; let him be slain treacherously by another, while he himself exercises the just sentence on Desdemona. He will destroy the beloved image because of the existence of the hated. Neither Hamlet nor Troilus had been confronted with this demand nor had it developed in themselves. Gertrude is not to be touched and Cressida is not even threatened. But neither were the heroes who had to deal with them so intensely conscious of their beauty. There goes up from Othello the most touching wail in all Shakespeare : 'Ay, let her rot, and perish, and be damned to-night, for she shall not live. . . O ! the world hath not a sweeter woman ; she might lie by an emperor's side, and command him tasks'—and so on. It is therefore that in the great act of the murder Desdemona is not killed until her unfortunate exclamation and tears change her before Othello's eyes into her other identity—the identity which overwhelms the perceptions of his love. It is also therefore that the sudden outburst of Emilia's intense sincerity destroys that identity in turn, and leaves him confronted with the fact that he has destroyed not merely the loved but the only Desdemona. He has been, literally, perplexed—perplexed as, long before, Adriana had been between the two Antipholuses ; to such a height of exquisite subtlety had the crude plot of the earlier play been carried. The Antipholuses were contradictory ; so were the Desdemonas. But one had been a contradiction of exterior laughter ; the other was of interior horror.

In *Othello*, however, the contradiction was between the beauty that had a soul and his contrary imagination of it. In *Lear* the contradiction is between the beauty that has no soul and Lear's contrary imagination. Othello's imagination is thrown into schism by deceit, but Lear's by fact. There would be hope, that is to say, for Othello, could true perception work. But there can be no hope for Lear once true perception has begun to work. Cordelia has been removed. Goneril and Regan are given no choice, or rather, their moral choice is not made part of the poetry. It does not therefore exist. We see them in action, but the action is the decision of their formed and determined natures.

It is perhaps not merely a joke to say that, in taking over the old *Leir* (as critics seem to agree that he did), Shakespeare left out everything that could make it reasonable or even credible. As if he were determined to leave no power but his own genius to work, he refused all help which he could have got from the story. The old play, as Tolstoy justly remarked, is a credible if not particularly probable story. The plot is carefully worked out, and the only rather forced moment is the appearance of the King of France in disguise. We must not count the opportune Murderer as a flaw, for Murderers were in Elizabethan literature even more common than they were in Elizabethan life, which seems to be saying a great deal. In those morally spacious days the highest spiritual and political authorities in Europe took a hand in the game of death with a realism inconceivable by our more puritanical generation, and a murderer more or less was neither here nor there unless controversial capital could be made out of it. The guilt for any particular murder or proposed murder may not have been where historians have placed it, but then the historians have been more disturbed about it than the actors. We have been anxious to provide them with innocence or excuse which it would not have occurred to them to require. The Murderer of *Leir* therefore is in every sense a homely figure, and even the disguised King of France is a conventional one. Outside those two figures the story is almost domestic—as indeed is Shakespeare's, here and in many other places. But Shakespeare never entirely dismissed royalty, however domestic the story; the crown was not for him so easily forgotten, and the chief cause of Kent being put in the stocks is to insult more flagrantly than could otherwise be done the messenger of a king, the equivalent of a herald, the inviolable representative of anointed Majesty. This is the cause of Kent's otherwise rather excessive violence towards Oswald in the castle of Cornwall; he has to be angry in order that he may be degraded, and the king with him. Possibly an Elizabethan audience would have thrilled to it more swiftly than we do.

But the old play was hardly so royal. It contained a more credible plot; it supplied more causes for Cordelia's banishment; it arranged that Regan should determine to have her father and his friend killed. In an open place the murderer finds them and threatens them. They entreat him; they seek to sacrifice, each himself for the other; and then in the sky is heard thunder. The murderer, terrified

of goodness, thunder, and the threat of hell, and
equating the last two, runs off. Lear and his friend
escape to the French king.

And if Shakespeare read the play he must have
seen all its opportunities—all, though perhaps some
were then only implicit. The king away from help
and comfort, the danger, the thunder—so much he
kept; from that centre he spun his own circle, as
if to show what could be done with the theme. The
one thing he did whole-heartedly accept was the
thunder. It is the storm which is the common
element in the plot of the old play and the poetry
of the new. In the old it is almost a character; its
crash is the Voice of Heaven. In the new it is more
nearly the condition in which a character moves; it
is the echo of the voice of earth, prolonged and re-
verberating through the state set up by the rest of
the poetry. 'The ghostly language of the antique
earth' which Wordsworth heard in the approaching
storm is here emphasizing the nature of earth; and
the 'great nature' which exists in this poetry involves
the duties and charities of natural relations as they
have been stabilized among men. It is the duty of
the old to protect and nourish the young; of the
young to reverence and protect the old: merely as
young and old. Youth has something to be served,
even if it be only youth; age something to be hon-
oured, though it be only age. But there is present
also a recognition of human laws established: primo-
geniture and royalty. The authority of natural
honour and of mortal honours combine; that which
is reverenced and outraged is the fact of man's
knowledge and ordering of nature. Edmund is the

natural first-born, but Edgar is the first-born in law, and that is what counts. It may or may not have been Shakespeare's personal decision; it is certainly here the method of his poetry. Lear himself incites the very outrage to which he is subjected, for he denies fidelity. It is the purest and clearest denial, unclouded by any question of new discoveries of fact. Lear has not even Cressida's excuse: his proposed indulgence is purely to his own freakish pleasure, already existing, unexcited by any external apparition. He determines his emotions, and for that he is prepared to deny the nature of things, the law even of the beasts, and the metaphysical nature of earth.

> For, by the sacred radiance of the sun,
> The mysteries of Hecate and the night,
> By all the operation of the orbs
> From whom we do exist and cease to be,
> Here I disclaim all my paternal care,
> Propinquity and property of blood,
> And as a stranger to my heart and me
> Hold thee from this for ever. The barbarous Scythian,
> Or he that makes his generation messes
> To gorge his appetite, shall to my bosom
> Be as well neighboured, pitied, and relieved,
> As thou my sometime daughter.

Only a hundred lines of the play have gone by when Cordelia invokes the duty she may one day owe her husband; nature will forbid her to 'love her father all'. Within the next twenty-two Lear has disclaimed that very nature, and invoked as witnesses the powers and operations which dictate that nature and instil it—'from whom we do exist and cease to be'. With that speech, almost with that line, there enters upon the stage the Nature of things as it is known in man's secular ordering of those experiences, especially of birth and death, and the propinquity of birth and death which we call youth and age.

This concentration on such Nature is brought about by a change from and accentuated doubly by comparison with *Othello*. The crisis there had been a crisis between Othello and Desdemona, between husband and wife. But in *Lear* it is a crisis between father and child, and again between father and child. The *kind* of relationship is changed into one more central to life, and the persons of that relationship are ostentatiously raised into symbolical figures. Destruction existing in sex is certainly a very terrible experience; it is, no doubt, more common and often more poignant than the ingratitude of children. But, to take a simple example of the difference between the themes, it is not so easy to use of it such a phrase as 'all germens spill at once That make ungrateful man'. The seed—which is the life—of man is not central to the tragedy in the one case as it is in the other. There was a time when Othello and Desdemona had been strangers; the exquisite 'magic' of their love depends on that, and partly by that the evil magic of Iago learns to work. The first scenes of the play are full of that strange magic. Brabantio even believes it to be actual sorcery. It is but the magic of natural and universal love, accentuated so that its wonder may be more thrilling and its overthrow more explicable. But there had never been a time when Goneril and Regan had been strangers to Lear; it is indeed only too probable, to look

outside the play, that he had been a 'proud father'.
All the exhortations of the physiologists have not
banished the delight of a lovely strangeness from
romantic love; a union of aliens is in its very
essence. But between fathers and children that experience need not exist; I do not say cannot. The
breach in the soul of man is in *Lear* manifested by
a breach in the seed of man.

The diction of the play insists on this schism
directly, but also it lifts its characters into it by a
process of which Cordelia's phrase may serve as an
example: 'Shall we not see These daughters and
these sisters?' Othello had never raised Desdemona
into the general category of 'wives'; the one individual was sufficient for his imagination. But in *Lear*
the general imagination is continually involving the
individual characters in relations almost philosophical by its use of words. Lear is a father; Goneril
and Regan are daughters. Others beside themselves
insist on it: 'his daughters seek his death'; 'he
childed as I father'd'; 'Tigers, not daughters . . . a
father, and a gracious aged man', so Gloucester,
Edgar, and Albany speak, and so continually.
Shakespeare was obviously content to raise his whole
contemplation of chaos into terms which would be
abstract were they not so terribly incarnated.

It is indeed upon the general and corporate influence of the words daughter and father and their
like, and of the words which involve the whole pro-
cesses of nature in the catastrophe that the poetry
of identity in this play depends. There are but
one scene and two brief speeches in which those
daughters are allowed to show the false identity in

which Lear so unprophetically believes ; after that
all is lost. It is not so much against what Goneril
and Regan were as against what they should be—
what, by all his knowledge of life, his adoration of
the great natural forces, his habitual belief in the
subordination of others to his fatherhood and king-
ship, they must be—that his new knowledge of what
they are is at war. Shakespeare had shown us in
Othello an imagined image of falsity contending with
the actual image of truth, but in *Lear* he reversed
this conflict, and gave us the actual image of falsity
contending with an imagined image of truth ; and
truth—as the play goes—not so much of memory as
of necessity. It would have been easy for him, had
he chosen, to present Lear as remembering the childhood or the obedience or the pretended amiability
of his daughters, but he never does ; he relies purely
on the nature of things in Lear's mind. Perception
is of this nature of things, incredibly outraged by
facts. But these facts are, after all, part of the nature
of things. It is by this means that he carries the
awareness of a contradiction and destruction beyond
the themes of *Hamlet* and *Troilus* and *Othello*. By
the fact also that whereas *Othello*, as was said just
now, depends on the creation of a false image of
destruction, here the image of destruction is actual,
and the dream of beauty false. Beauty has not
merely lost her soul ; she never had a soul. Troilus
and Othello do not deny their past experiences of
beauty, however that beauty is changed, and the new
wonder of its change discovered by their poetry. But
Lear discovers, one might say, a yet further wonder :
that from the beginning this is what beauty was; he

has had daughters, and this is what daughters are. The word daughter signifies a living outrage upon paternity. We approach the discovery that the rule in unity itself is a dreadful and callous rule; and man cannot suffer it. This is the poetry

> Wherein as in a mirror we behold
> The highest reaches of a human wit.

And even discursive reasoning has its part to play and its perceptions to create. Goneril and Regan, interestingly enough, have but one unreasonable scene—the first, and their irrational flatteries are rebuked by Cordelia's logic.

> Why have my sisters husbands if they say
> They love you all?

After their outbursts, with the exception of a brief farewell to their sister, they are silent till they are alone; then they turn from poetry to prose, and from exposition to reasoning. 'Since our father is thus infirm', in effect they argue, 'we are likely to suffer from his infirmity ; the more as that infirmity increases with his years. We shall, by his abdication and unconstant starts of authority, be worse off than before. It is therefore necessary for us to hold together and to take immediate action.'

In this extremely reasonable attitude they continue. 'Lear,' says Goneril, 'still wants to manage those authorities "which he hath given away". But he cannot; he has given them away. He must therefore be checked ; measures must be taken with him which would be shameful except that necessity compels them. Let him, to avoid this, remedy faults ; that is to say, let him diminish his train, and

let those that remain be grave and aged men.'
Coming directly after Lear's tumultuous demand
for immediate dinner, this sweet reasonableness is
accentuated ; or would be, if it were not that we
are too conscious of Goneril's power and intention,
by her use of words which convey almost the physical force they threaten.

> Be then desired
> By her that else will take the things she begs.

But she does not take it yet ; that appalling reasonableness has another scene to live through, where it
knows itself more clearly. It opens there with one
of the most reasonable—and most terrible—lines in
the play, when Goneril arrives at Gloucester's castle
and the two daughters, confronting their father—
still brooding over the herald of his royalty in
degradation—utter themselves in Regan's realistic
phrase—'I pray you, father, being weak, seem so.'
She repeats the sense afterwards.

> Those that mingle reason with your passion
> Must be content to know you old ;

and there follows the reasonable reduction—fifty ;
five-and-twenty,—what need five-and-twenty, ten,
five ? 'What need one ?'

He answers, he breaks into the protest : 'O reason
not the need', but it and he are impotent against
the exact reasoning faculty and the power in action
of that beauty which has no soul, and, now it seems,
never, never had. He rushes out ; and the scene
closes with a line which in its flat common sense,
its consummation of ordinary selfish intelligence,
is a fit continuance and conclusion of Regan's whole

mind. The tempest is breaking over the earth and the heath; what does one do when it rains? Take shelter. The final grasp of that reasonable fact is given to Regan's husband. The Duke of Cornwall realizes that it is raining—

My Regan counsels well; come out o' the storm.

i.e, no sense of the pattern?

Beauty without a soul, and having therefore nothing but its own immediate interests by which to measure all relations—as daughter or as wife or as subject—has its own proper perceptive reason and its own power. Power has been handed over to it by an imagination of the right relations of things, though in such a surrender that imagination itself has been false to its knowledge. Goneril and Regan would have had no power at all against Lear unless he himself had given it to them; perhaps, in this sense, having so delivered it, he had the original and greater sin though his own nature was less coldly evil. Let the memory of Wordsworth's definition be pressed one step further. As the unsouled Beauty has reason and now power, so had the right imagination. But the power of Imagination is now impotent; its vision of beauty has been by its own will exiled or thereafter against its own will removed; and its reason becomes incoherent. Its perception, that is to say, begins to lose its own capacity. Gloucester wishes he were distraught;

So should my thoughts be severed from my griefs,
And woes by wrong imaginations lose
The knowledge of themselves.

This is the definition of the climax which in *Lear*

we are always approaching. Imagination, by which we know our griefs and woes, through its perceptiveness, is all but lost in wrong imagination. Not quite; for the play is a play, and must have interest and harmony. If Lear lost entire relation to things we should lose interest in him; he is led to the verge but stayed where Edgar can say

> O matter and impertinency mixed!
> Reason in madness!

But Imagination which goes so far in contemplating woes losing knowledge of themselves in wrong imaginations—so far and with such power of poetry —has gone near the contemplation of its own destruction. And since the evidence and speech of Imagination is poetry, here the power of poetry is devoted, as it were, to the extinction of power. Lear's own self-loss arises from his sense of 'the general curse' that nature has been brought to, but it arouses in us, however undefined, a remoter sense of a cataclysm in poetry. The imagination of Shakespeare here rightly contemplated all 'wrong imaginations' and held them steady. We are never allowed to lose the knowledge of ourselves, though that knowledge here contained the possibility of its own destruction. To express that it had to put out all its power; it had never been greater than now.

And then, as if Shakespeare had determined to try to discover how Goneril and Regan became indeed Goneril and Regan, we return to choice. Those sisters and daughters had existed already full-grown. But in what way is it possible for them to have grown? The answer is *Macbeth*. Lear had betrayed fidelity to the nature of things in a sudden fit of unwise rage—Macbeth does it deliberately. Lear had discovered something which contradicted through every fibre of his being the nature of things as he believed it to be, and had gone mad. But Macbeth, having separated himself from that nature of things as he believed it to be, is to be left to his chosen separation. We return not merely to sanity but to continued sanity. Macbeth is not to go mad, because that would be to lose the whole exploration of the play ; which is to discover a mind accepting a false imagination for truth, and then seeking to impose it on the true imagination—knowingly. Macbeth is in the end to find himself so wedded to a false universe, or rather to *no* universe, that he has no place even for his dearest partner. Lady Macbeth did well to die ; she had lost her husband to a lonelier bridal.

But Macbeth's choice of sin (to use theological language) is still to be expressed in the Shakespearian idiom of poetry: that is, it will be expressed by the language of natural things, and not supernatural, and (from the present point of view) in terms of changed identity. That Macbeth does not originally contemplate the change which actually takes place is true enough. But he contemplates a change in his powers and in his imagination of himself and his powers. It is this contemplation which is his beginning in the play. What on earth does it matter whether he had or had not discussed the murder with Lady Macbeth before the play began (except for the fun we can get out of talking

about it) ? The great fact is revealed to us in the
line of the Third Witch :

All hail, Macbeth ! that shalt be king hereafter.

There exists then—for him and for us—the image
of himself as king, the new identity which is revealed
to him and which he loves. In the other plays the
separation between identities had led to action or to
madness ; but this is to involve (as he sees it) reconciliation. The present time is to be united with
the prophecy. Lady Macbeth's phrase is exactly
right ; he also feels 'the future in the instant'. The
instant therefore, and the following instants, will
devote themselves to the future already felt. But it
is just there that Macbeth's own difficulty lies. He
has accepted the 'strange intelligence', the 'prophe-
tic greeting'; 'nothing is But what is not'. But the
perfect harmony of what is with what is not, though
it is clear to his perception, is refused by his choice.
The most difficult problem of all poetry was before
Shakespeare ; it was that which confronted Milton
in Satan—to show the operation of choice in the
farthest profundity possible to poetry. Macbeth
himself does not want to see it ;

Yet let that be
Which the eye fears, when it is done, to see,

and the more before it is done. But as the Witches
showed him the end, so Lady Macbeth shows him
the means. The hindrances are the same humanities
that measured *Lear*—the natural order of the universe as formulated by man : the 'double trust' of
kinsman and subject; the virtues of Duncan; pity;
the golden opinions of men. But these perceptions

cannot coexist with that perception of himself as
other and more than what he is ; he refuses them ;
he desires to identify himself with the vision of
himself as king. Such an identification involves also
identification of himself with the means, and in
the end his choice is made, as it were sideways. He
slides away from the question 'Am I to use these
means ? ' to 'Will these means succeed ? ' 'If we
should fail—'. Convinced that they need not fail,
he finds that he has accepted the unfailing means.
The 'I dare not' in his mind is imperceptibly turned
into another 'I dare not'; the first involved morality,
the second danger. He turns from a moral to a
material objection, and in that turning his choice
is made ; the deed is already done. Convinced that
the danger does not exist, he finds that nature has
disappeared also.

> I am settled, and bend up
> Each corporal agent to this terrible feat.

Murder is no longer to be fantastical. The terrible
harmony of Lady Macbeth's perceptive reason has
its way, and both of them behold their other imagined identities as forced upon the world, and the
world accepting them. 'Who dares receive it
other ? '

There follows the scene of the murder. And as in
Othello Shakespeare withdrew from the direct alteration to the indirect, so here he withdraws from
direct to indirect death. Desdemona might be slain
on the stage but not Duncan. Verbal poetry must
do the work. He relaxed afterwards in the killing
of Banquo, but that is a lesser moment. Lady
Macbeth unconsciously described the moment in

her phrase about the grooms—'death and nature do contend'. The outrage upon nature in *Lear* had broken into madness, but there is no madness here. There is not even a storm. It is true that in the next scene we hear that 'the night has been unruly', but in the court of the castle Lady Macbeth has heard the owl scream and the crickets cry, and the chimneys that were blown down where Lennox lay left the peace of that secret dialogue undisturbed. By talk, and only by talk, the universe is changed. Blessing is destroyed; sleep is destroyed; the 'chief nourisher in life's feast'—the phrase which moves Lady Macbeth to that extremely difficult cry 'What do you mean ?'—is destroyed ; the ocean is incarnadined. This again, as in *Lear*, is nature feeling

> the general curse
> Which twain have brought her to.

And Macbeth, as the curse falls, knows the curse, and knows that to escape it ' 'twere best not know myself'. But that is done ; he has chosen how to know himself, and for the rest of the play he must know himself so. Ross, thinking of the suspicion that has fallen on the princes, exclaims

> 'Gainst nature still !
> Thriftless ambition, that wilt ravin up
> Thine own life's means !

It is a phrase which would have been peculiarly applicable to them, had they been guilty; it applies to the daughters of another play. Goneril and Regan had ravined up their own lives' means. But as Goneril and Regan had carried into an enlarged experience of mortal relations the vision which

Othello had of Desdemona, so Macbeth universalizes that experience yet more entirely. He is become life ravening on itself. The centre of the play therefore is not so much the struggle between two worlds, the bitter awareness of conflicting identities, as one world eating up itself. The identities of Macbeth have become cannibal. His hunger spreads from Duncan to destroy Banquo and Fleance, to rage at Macduff, to bestow on 'feasts and banquets bloody knives', and comes at last to the terrible command in the cavern of the weird sisters.[1] If that command is compared with Lear's invocations, it will be seen how far we have passed beyond the wild prayers of madness.

> Blow, winds, and crack your cheeks! rage! blow!
> You cataracts and hurricanoes, spout
> Till you have drench'd our steeples, drown'd the cocks!
> You sulphurous and thought-executing fires,
> Vaunt-couriers to oak-cleaving thunderbolts,
> Singe my white head! And thou, all-shaking thunder,
> Strike flat the thick rotundity o' the world!
> Crack nature's moulds, all germens spill at once
> That make ingrateful man![2]

Macbeth. How now, you secret, black, and midnight hags! What is't you do?
All.　　　　　A deed without a name.
Macbeth. I conjure you, by that which you profess,—

[1] Whom now Macbeth knows where to find. It is, no doubt, Shakespeare being casual; originally Macbeth knew nothing of their dwelling. But it would have been suitable enough that he should now find his way there without difficulty.

[2] One might see in *Othello* the sulphurous and thought-executing fire that is a vaunt-courier to the thunderbolt of *Lear* striking the world flat.

Howe'er you come to know it,—answer me :
Though you untie the winds and let them fight
Against the churches ; though the yesty waves
Confound and swallow navigation up ;
Though bladed corn be lodg'd and trees blown down ;
Though castles topple on their warders' heads ;
Though palaces and pyramids do slope
Their heads to their foundations ; though the treasure
Of Nature's germens tumble all together,
Even till destruction sicken ; answer me
To what I ask you.

There is a difference between the two, and the
difference is the measure between Lear desiring the
destruction of himself and life and Macbeth desiring
his own preservation at the cost of the destruction
of life. But this he cannot have ; all he can do is to
destroy, for himself, all meaning in life. Poetry,
expanding to its full conclusion, devours existence.
Life signifies nothing. Life has fed on itself till it
has already sickened.

I 'gin be aweary of the sun
And wish the estate of the world were now undone.

There was to be an answer to that when Florizel
declared to Perdita that every one of her actions was
perfect—'all your acts are queens', as if each moment
was entirely sufficient in itself, and signified enough
in utterly signifying itself. The last comedies may
have been faerie or truth ; but, as far as their poetry
goes, it is not less powerful than that of Macbeth's
despair. It has been pointed out that they are concerned again with youth, and in youth with the high
power and awful perception of love. There may be
added to that the fact that nowhere in them does

Shakespeare modify, excuse, or deprecate such
capacities of love. Nothing is more common than
for older people to shake sympathetic heads over the
presence of young love, to imply—however sadly—
that it will not last or cannot be relied on ; that its
identity will change, and its vision be lost. Maturity
is almost bound to insinuate caution. For what it
is worth, it may be remarked that the genius of
the greatest of our poets in the full exercise of its
power never found a mighty phrase to subdue that
young vision. It created phrase after phrase of delighted perception of it; it created old people who
forgot or destroyed it, but it kept those separate.
Posthumus is the only lover who is allowed to be
bothered by a supposed alteration, and Shakespeare
caused him to repent upon his next appearance and
before he learns the truth. He only disbelieves for
Imogen's sake, that her clarity may be the better
shown. The maturity of Shakespeare's genius confirmed the dreams of youth. In *The Tempest* he
brought even the simplicity of young love to its
final simplicity. He chose to find language for
Miranda. There could be no state of love more
easily mocked by the wise world than that of the
first love of a girl who had never yet seen a young
man. Shakespeare delayed to allow Prospero to
point this out just sufficiently, so that we cannot
suppose himself ignorant of it. But knowing it, he
confirmed its beauty.

> I might call him
> A thing divine, for nothing natural
> I ever saw so noble.

> There's nothing ill can build in such a temple.

Dryden and Davenant doubled and tripled that simplicity and spoiled it; for its simplicity is in its singleness, and to double singleness is to lose it. Between the double images of the identical thing, incredulity, ridicule, crudity, can make their appearance. As if in answer to Miranda's singleness Ferdinand perceived at once the fire and frost which love creates—

> The white-cold virgin snow upon my heart
> Abates the ardour of my liver;

either delighting in the other and in the contrast.

It is a non-poetic comment, except in so far as that great style chose to attempt a perfection of existence in which existence is utterly sufficient for itself. That he used romantic love for it is of no direct poetic importance, however much we may be disposed to believe that his choice was actuated by the truth of things. But it is of some poetic value that he should attempt a perception of pure beauty, or as near pure beauty as man (outside the supernatural) knows, and that his style became pellucid for his need.

But before the last comedies there was *Antony and Cleopatra*. And *Coriolanus* and *Timon*. In all of these the problem of identity appears, but its chief place is in *Antony*. Not only is *Antony* the greatest play of these three, but it is so—partly, at least—because it achieves a particular kind of totality to which the others make no pretence. It is not too much to say that *Antony* is unique, even in Shakespeare, in its method. It is the only one among the greater plays which comes near to presenting itself with an equal intensity from everybody's point of view; which is not to say that one particular point of view is not more important than the others. There can be very little doubt that the poetry of the play reaches a climax in the death of Cleopatra, and in her own knowledge of herself in death. The other states of knowledge are forgotten in that supreme couple of hundred lines. But nevertheless they have been there ; they have, each of them, been part of the play, and the play might—up to that abounding climax—have agreed with any of them. It does not.

Elsewhere, even when alternative agreements were offered, they were not offered in such high poetry. In *Hamlet*, for example, the play itself is not seen through the eyes of Claudius or Gertrude, of Polonius or Horatio, not even of Ophelia. We are no doubt presented with poetry which expresses Ophelia's view of Hamlet himself. But that poetry reflects on Ophelia even more than on Hamlet ; except for an occasional heightening of the pathos it does not illumine the whole theme of the play ; certainly it does not give us a view of the whole theme which is alternative to and exclusive of Hamlet's own view. And except for Ophelia there is no view of the play but Hamlet's—whatever view of his character we take. Our judgement of the action depends on our judgement of him, and vice versa, but we are restrained to him. In *Othello* again we do not find our apprehension of Othello in danger of change when we read the poetry of Desdemona; that only confirms our feeling about him and about Iago. Nor indeed does Othello's mistaken view of Iago affect ours. All the poetry

of all the play moves upon one aspect of its theme
and upon one method of value. In *Lear*, though we
are shown Goneril's view of her father, and Regan's,
yet again that is done so that we realize more intensely the dereliction of Lear which his own poetry
offers us : and so with Albany's speeches. In *Macbeth* both Macbeth himself and the undistinguished
thanes who overthrow him agree on the kind of man
that he is and the kind of thing that is happening.
The approach of Birnam Wood does not alter—it
only emphasizes the double somnambulism of Dun-
sinane. But in *Antony* the single light is countershot
by others. In the other plays we had seen everybody's point of view, but here we see the whole
play from everybody's point of view, or at least from
quite a number—from Cleopatra's and Antony's
and Caesar's and Enobarbus's, and even (for a single
scene) from the Soothsayer's. All these persons are
not merely persons; they are poetic powers. They
project their own potentialities upon the main theme
and it is this which helps to make the complexity
of the play. Cleopatra is, in another sense, 'every
man's Cleopatra'; for in this play Shakespeare gave
intense life to all that could be said against her, and
answered it again from some other region. He
even multiplies denunciation, and that in the grand
style ; just as he defines Caesar by Caesar's judgement as well as the judgements of the lovers. He
does here for the theme of the one play what he
did throughout all the plays for life itself ; utters
every kind of poetry about it and then carries it into
a last state of simple being. It is perhaps why
Cleopatra seems so to reflect life itself; to be, could

we so interfere, by an extreme interpretation, with
unknown genius, a symbol of life itself. But that
way the wilder subjective madnesses lie ; let us keep
to objective poetry.

This universality of vision, by which so steady a
centre is seen in such changing lights, is largely
due to the extraordinary economy of the play. It
has been admired for its magniloquence, its scope,
its distances and periods—and justly ; the capacity
which so easily commanded such things can hardly
be too much adored. But perhaps we have not quite
sufficiently noted its economy—of phrase, of movement, of conclusion. The speed of the play is too
great for us ; compacted states of being follow each
·other, and one 'treads on another's heels'. The
phrases are among the most compressed in Shakespeare ; they follow *Macbeth* in their kind.

> O my oblivion is a very Antony
> And I am all forgotten !

is an example of a saying which would take paragraphs to paraphrase, and less complex sentences
have a yet greater economy about them.

> Now
> All length is torture ;

the experience there is terrible in its compression.

> All's but naught ;
> Patience is sottish, and impatience does
> Become a dog that's mad,

is again a poetic economy of the highest rank.
And so with all the mixed 'metaphors'; let us admit
the mixing—it is their glory.

> The hearts
> That spaniell'd me at heels, to whom I gave
> Their wishes, do discandy, melt their sweets
> On blossoming Caesar.

The style of *Antony* makes magnificence itself economical; it is the supreme example of magniloquence
which is itself but meiosis of experience.

And if the diction is economical so also is the
movement. The play darts from this city to that;
countries are shown for a moment and then with-
drawn; armies and navies gleam and vanish. But
it is for the moment and the gleam that they are
there; they are the quickest and briefest method
of displaying the chameleon-shaded central image.
But the chameleon tints are nevertheless those of the
varying backgrounds, not of that image. The brief
scene in which Ventidius appears has been explained
as being a satirical comment upon the masters of
the world and their jealousy. But if we take Ventidius merely as the expression of an abstract comment
we lose vitality; it is Ventidius's own colour flung
on Antony.

> Ambition,
> The soldier's virtue, rather makes choice of loss
> Than gain which darkens him.

He is cautious and bitter because he is ambitious;
his foresight for himself provides his insight into
Antony. Self-regard is reflected from both. It is
the envious fault in Antony's thirst for glory, cor-
respondent to the egotism of Cleopatra; but his
other servants do not observe it, only the ambitious
man. Also, it is the first spiritual desertion—no

doubt provoked by Antony's fault, but in its detached critical judgement none the less a desertion from Antony. Ventidius does not want to please Antony; he wants to save himself. It is a double realism, and it is the prelude of Canidius and Enobarbus, lightly touched at the very height of victorious splendour. But its effect is a little lost if we suppose Ventidius to be only the unselfish instead of the selfish soldier.

Lear had declared itself (by Edgar's comment on Lear) to be 'reason in madness' and there is a phrase in *Antony* which describes it in turn. 'If you can', says Antony to the Soothsayer, 'your reason?' And the Soothsayer darkly answers:

> I see it in
> My motion, have it not in my tongue.

We cannot say that *Antony* has not its reason in its tongue, but that is because its motion is there also. But its motion lies in the changing effects of all the tongues, in the way they challenge and answer each other. Poetry flies from one to another, but by that continual flight—athwart and thwarting itself —it yet proceeds towards the single end. The play opens with a challenge it sets itself to answer.

> You shall see in him
> The triple pillar of the world transformed
> Into a strumpet's fool.

Against that, and the preceding lines, the dialogue between the lovers is but the rant of lust. But the rant is to become literal truth, and to defeat by its truth the accusation that was originally the truer utterance.

Then must thou needs find out new heaven, new earth.

Eros!—I come, my queen!—Eros!—Stay for me
Where souls do couch on flowers we'll hand in hand
And with our sprightly port make the ghosts gaze.

Husband, I come!

To that final conclusion the movement of the play
had taken its way, but it had never forgotten anything. Right to the very end Shakespeare again and
again pressed home everything that could be said
in derogation of the lovers.

> I found you as a morsel cold upon
> Dead Caesar's trencher.

Neither Cleopatra nor Antony has any contradiction in their view of each other. They know each
other almost entirely, but they do not know their
passion, nor life, nor that their passion is all but
one with life—that is, with the movement of Shakespeare's determination of life here and thus. The
poetry of the play determines the kind of conclusion
it will have, and that breaks out in its full force
when Mardian brings the false news of Cleopatra's
death. Antony moves in twenty-three words from
the illusions of his self-consciousness to the truth of
his consciousness.

> She hath betrayed me and shall die the death!
>
>   . . . Dead then?
>
> Unarm, Eros; the long day's task is done,
> And we must sleep.

'All length is torture'; the twenty lines in which
that phrase occurs are so long to him that when
again he speaks to any but himself, he begins with

a phrase of the 'infinite tedium'—which Macbeth had known—'Since Cleopatra died'.

But it was for Cleopatra herself, with all her faults and follies on her, 'nothing extenuated', that Shakespeare preserved an even further exploration; by her mouth he defined their mutual and common catastrophe more closely, in a phrase as profound as any he ever used—'The odds is gone'.

> Young boys and girls
> Are level now with men; the odds is gone,
> And there is nothing left remarkable
> Beneath the visiting moon.

It is not merely the rhetoric of grief; it is the last intellectually exact contradiction of reason, the lesser and the greater reason—Euclid and Snowdon. For it denies all importance by denying all proportion. Antony had been but a moment earlier the 'noblest of men'; his death would leave the world 'no better than a sty'. That was very well three lines before. But when he is dead, it is the very means of discovering nobility and the difference between the world and a sty that has vanished. There is no sense of any kind of value left at all; therefore no significance. The awareness of Macbeth and of Cleopatra for a single second are in touch. But there had been a difference; Macbeth had been full of an intense vision of himself, Cleopatra— more than she knew—of an intense vision of Antony. Macbeth's vitality recedes, but Cleopatra's enters a new state of being.

She swoons by the side of the dead triumvir. It is so easy to read oneself into Shakespeare disproportionately—something of the sort we must do—

that I feel bound to half-apologize for the extreme value here attached to this moment. It is, of course, wrong. But since any kind of interpretation of poetry at this pitch must be wrong, perhaps it is no more wrong than any, and it is certainly not meant in any sense exclusively. She swoons, and with her recovery Shakespeare's poetry entered on its last sublime movement, a sublimity soon to be touched by laughter into the clarity of which there had been a single promise in *Lear*.

> Think that the clearest gods, who make them honours
> Of men's impossibilities, have preserved thee.

So Edgar had exhorted Gloucester. The clearest gods of poetry were making themselves honours now; they were beginning to reflect themselves into Shakespeare's whole style. Irony disappears—almost entirely—from this and all future plays; irony which had had its greatest public ostentation in Antony's earlier oration in *Julius Caesar*. Cleopatra awakes to the elemental facts of her being; in the final comedies Shakespeare had but to carry that great simplicity on.

The perceptions in this play then are of two kinds: (i) those which all the chief characters have of the centre, (ii) those which Antony and Cleopatra have of themselves. And the remarkable thing about those perceptions—about that Reason—is that we can no longer use pairs of words like right and wrong or true and false about either the perceptions or that which they perceive. They are all true, and yet none of them is true—until the death-swoon of Cleopatra. It is then her own perception which becomes the play—the clouding of it, and the clearing of it; and that perception is occupied with the immediate movement. She sees what she is and what others are, and her women rise with her.

> He words me, girls, he words me . . .

> Finish, good lady; the bright day is done,
> And we are for the dark.

The almost negligible Iras is given that perception. It is against that great cluster of perceptive clarities that the Guard are permitted the distracted muddle of the outer world looking on the perceiving integrities of death:

> Approach ho! All's not well; Caesar's beguiled.

To be fair, Caesar was wiser:

> Caesar, thy thoughts
> Touch their effects in this;

and he deserved his own lesser lines, with their more common perception, and yet noble:

> She looks like sleep
> As she would catch another Antony
> In her strong toil of grace.

In a sense, however, when the concern with right and wrong, the moral concern, is past, we come back to what may be fairy-tales, or may be the union of beauty and truth. It is, of course, true that in the final comedies, there are persons who, we feel, behave undesirably: Leontes, Posthumus and the Queen, Alonzo and Sebastian and Antonio. But, compared with *Macbeth*, we are not allowed to worry much even during the play, over their moral behaviour, and at the end of the play, we are not to worry at all. Every one is either conveniently killed or happily forgiven. I am by no means convinced that Shakespeare was not perfectly well aware how easily he was treating his plots, or that he cared anything about plots. Away behind him lay the early plays, in which words had followed—sometimes at great length—an intellectual meaning, and the intellectual meaning had described the characters. Romeo is known by the speeches he delivers, and his speeches intelligibly express what he wants to say. They are, as it were, grammatical. But in the later plays the poetry had turned to more exalted labour; it had compressed itself, it had taken its grammar into the place of its own Shakespearian idiom, and it had been greatly concerned with men's relationships with themselves, with each other, and with things. Rational thought had given way to verbal thought; the 'mixed metaphors' arise, when necessary, because the words are more important than logical sequence. But the violence and tragedy of those plays arises from a sense of contending identities, provoked by men's relationships; and—to an extent —those relationships are the plots. In the last plays the plots—and therefore the relationships—dwindle in importance. They are at best but a thread which can conveniently draw together whatever kind of poetry Shakespeare happened to be writing. The poetry has abandoned even relationships except as means by which the poetry of absolute states of being exist. As Posthumus is to Imogen, as the bear to Antigonus, as the magical island to Miranda, so are all the plots to all the poetry: a convenience lightly taken. The poetry concentrates on absolute identities. In the chief characters, changes of identity do not occur. Change of temper may; change of spirit never. Never except when it does: there is Leontes. But Shakespeare did not bother much about Leontes's conversion; he wrote in a little scene which made Delphi and the God curiously convincing to us, and then at the height of the excitement at the trial caused Leontes to defy the God. Rather unkindly, he also killed Mamilius at that moment, in order to convert Leontes without any further bother. Which he does of course—and us to the conversion. But all natures and identities of beauty he maintains to the end; he causes beauty to be truth and truth beauty by the almost indolent exercise of his genius. At the end, he raised up Miranda and Ariel; he closed each of them in a perfection of existence and left it there.

Such were the kindred mutations he sent abroad over and through the universe. His absolute power exercised its insight, its amplitude, its exaltation; and of the moments in which it does so it may be said, as Florizel said of Perdita, that 'all its acts are queens'. To believe that life is like that—that all the acts of life are queens—is a matter for a decision that is not poetry's. But, if indeed, such a decision is possible, the pure experience of Shakespeare's style may purify us to apprehend those acts as his genius seems in the end to have done—'so singular in each particular'—and Reason in its most exalted mood may unite our own styles of living with the style of that great verse.

X

THE DISPERSAL OF MIST

A COMPLETE study of Reason in the progressive achievements of poetry would involve a much longer and a much more pretentious book than the present, since there is, of course, no English poet of any value who has not his own style, and in his style his own unique perceptions. The arrangement and harmony of his more immediate perceptions—of what Wordsworth called his insight—is that which makes up his Reason in its own most exalted mood; more accurately, it is his Reason in that mood which directs and controls his insight until, after its own method, it reaches its 'Composure and ennobling Harmony'. The 'absolute power' of each poet is absolute to its own degree; and in that degree it expresses itself in the three dimensions which Wordsworth defined—insight, knowledge ('amplitude of mind'), and reason. The present essays have been concerned only to mark several stages of that absolute power; each stage absolute within itself, and yet each discovered to be less than the greater state which expands beyond it. The two chief lines of inquiry which need to be followed in order to correct or confirm them are (i) the inclusion of other poets, (ii) the investigation of the style—in its more limited sense—of the greater poets, a close consideration of their varying diction and rhythms, their metaphors and epigrams, their pauses and silences. But the first would enlarge the book past bearing; the second would require a different kind of book.

The mere form of verse helps to impose upon us the vivid sensation of a power dealing with such 'compass of the universe' as is allowed to it. The 'glorious faculties' of those powers vary; 'one star differeth from another in glory', as—using the same word that Wordsworth used—the Authorized Version declared. Each of them, however, sends abroad over the universe 'mutations' from itself kindred to the universe, and creates for itself 'a like existence'. Its power, and the measure of its power, is known by the kind of existence it creates. The words 'kindred mutations' might, not unfairly, be taken to describe the process of poetry. Poetry shifts and varies as does the universe itself; those variations being known by its varying insight, and amplitude, and harmony of diverse perceptions. Marlowe, seeking the definition of poetry after his own manner, told us that there was always something it could not include. In the mirror of the highest reaches of a human wit there would always be something not reflected. It was easier for Marlowe to say so than for us, for he lived before Shakespeare and Milton and Wordsworth. He may have been right nevertheless; even *Macbeth* and *Paradise Lost*, *The Tempest* and *Samson*, may leave something untold. Yet we do not feel in some of their august lines the same sense of limitation or insufficiency which we feel in Pope or Spenser. But that is because Pope and Spenser suffer from comparison with them; without the greater we might be more contented with the lesser. Bearing this in mind we must admit that, in the abstract, Marlowe may be right; even Shakespeare and Milton may be overpassed.

Indeed, the only excuse for a single new poem is that it has in mind to overpass them at some point. We should possibly lessen our own flow of verse if we questioned, before we published, whether the thing were not already more adequately shaped in them. But this is a counsel of sanctity in letters, and, even so, perhaps not to be too strictly taken. We need not too carefully avoid any small new pleasure of verse because Shakespeare has already put it in its place in half of some odd line, or Milton in some normally-neglected adjective. We do not —yet—live by the masters; when we do, our own oblivion will be even more easily obtained than it is now.

They being our greatest, we can see in their light the thoughts, graces, and wonders which the virtue of the lesser poets has not digested into words. It seems that those two deal with the *whole* compass of the universe, merely by showing forth the nature of their style. The harmony of perception in style was described by Wordsworth in another passage.

> Dust as we are, the immortal spirit grows
> Like harmony in music; there is a dark
> Inscrutable workmanship that reconciles
> Discordant elements, makes them cling together
> In one society.

The reconciliation of discordant elements is one of the chief tasks which poetry sets before itself in mutations kindred to those which the mere business of life imposes, more or less effectively, on us. The 'use' of poetry, if the word were not misleading, is that its harmony can induce harmony. The word is apt to be misleading because it seems to subdue poetry to our needs, instead of subduing our needs to poetry. We quote poetry (God forgive us!) because it expresses what we believe to be our emotions or our thoughts, and Macbeth or Samson are used to body forth our momentary moods. The 'thrill' of poetry, unexplored and misunderstood, encourages us to believe that those moods are of so great a nature, or indeed greater, since we can use the divine phrases for our self-definition. But it is not so; we are neither Macbeths nor Samsons—no, nor even the Divine Son or Hamlet. Poetry has to rebuke that folly as well as many another before its pure nature can work on our minds, and we may venture to let our 'kindred mutations' modestly correspond to its own. We are subordinated to it; like Adam and Eve, we adore and obey the Reason, Power, and Beauty which are to be freely served and freely loved. In that sense a regained paradise is open to us.

But certainly poetry, having only men's experiences to work on, discovers in its material the discordant elements of which it there spoke, and has to do something about them. The poets here considered present different methods of operation. There is the method of discursive reasoning which Pope followed. But the arguments of the *Essay on Man* are destroyed by Pope's own genius of insight, if not by his amplitude of mind ; he negatives by his own passion for actuality what he asserts by the borrowed intelligence of Lord Bolingbroke. In our own day another philosophical poem—more intellectually satisfying than the *Essay*—has been given

us: *The Testament of Beauty.* The *Testament* has an
amplitude greater than Pope's, though perhaps its
immediate insight is less piercing; it moves us
sometimes more nobly, sometimes more warmly, but
as a general rule without that fervour of mortal
recognition which Pope could launch at any moment.
Its subject is the transmutation of man's instincts
into his Reason and the exaltation of that Reason into
an apprehension of divinity. In some sense therefore
it lays down the whole ground plan of poetry, and it
—or many parts of it—may be better read in relation
to the poetic genius than to our life itself, as it so
greatly pretends. To that hypothetical reading there
are too many difficulties of disagreement. In philosophical poetry one cannot neglect the immediate
moral argument. But in the greatest poetry one is
always aware that the human element is greater even
than the moral element. Even if a changing moral
system were to decide that Macbeth was perfectly
justified in killing Duncan, it would still remain true
that the play is a terrible process of a man's separation from the living universe; we could pretend
ourselves back into its own moral state and realize
its mortal catastrophe. But this is—I will not say
impossible but much more difficult in such a poem
as the *Testament.* Its perceptions are abstracted
even from such a history of a mind as the *Prelude*
presents; it turns, as so much English verse has
so beautifully done, to reverie rather than to action.
'The nightmare Life-in-Death', the skeleton that
walks in English verse, is to be seen at a distance
only, and though the rhythms of that poem are
anything but prosaic, yet perhaps its total conclusion

leaves us directed rather towards the dominion of prose than of poetry.

The *Testament* lies in its whole style (from the present point of view) between Pope and Spenser. It maintains an argument like the one in a habit of speech which is more like the other. It is not perhaps very like even so, but its beauties and exquisite vignettes are distantly related to those other intervolved beauties, even though Spenser lost hold of his allegory more completely than Bridges of his doctrine. The one lack common to all three poets—without admitting any derogation from the peculiar honour of each—is the essence of tragedy. And unless discordant elements are not merely addressed towards but compelled on to tragedy, how can their discordance be utterly known? It might be said that Hardy does precisely drive his elements to tragedy, and that is true enough; but his elements are hardly discordant. They hurry, they run, to tragedy; they will have no other trysting-place. They do not analyse the very dichotomy which they deplore in others. His gospel is multitudinous, but it is single; the pale identity of beauty wanders wraith-like and aware that she is only a wraith. Beauty has perhaps everywhere to be discovered not to be truth, but when we all know so certainly from the beginning that she is not, there is less terror in discovering it. That does not merely mean that Hardy's poems repeat themselves; they do, but that is not the point. It is a remote and improper, though natural, objection that no poet ought to have known all about it from the beginning; his genius should obey the laws of growth. But it is not so improper to say that Hardy's style confines itself to sadness and to a reverie of sadness. So many things happen and yet hardly anything happens ; the verse retires into itself and avoids the awful dispute of the soul. And even if there is not and never has been such a dispute, yet the imagination of it is something which must be transcended by a passionate perception of its annihilation. Hardy did not annihilate ; he shook his head. That would be well enough if (let us say) Milton and Shakespeare had never written. But the existence of Milton and Shakespeare made Hardy's reverie seem more tenderly sad than he altogether meant. A good deal of his verse is Troilus or Satan being less intellectual and much more pathetic, not to say self-pathetic, than on their original appearances. The *Dynasts* is one of our finest philosophical poems. Its reason, within its own measure, is complete. But as its manner of diction avoids all ostentation of beauty and confines itself to a quiet meiosis, so its manner of thought avoids the living skeleton of anguish by merely sitting on the sepulchre of delight. Joy there is already in its grave, and is not allowed to rise—not even as a vampire.

It is the vampire of joy, 'the nightmare Life-in-Death', which Shakespeare, more than any of our poets, imagined in his work, and it is his definition of it in *Troilus* which has been taken as the centre of these essays. That is not, of course, to say that *Troilus* is the only place where a particular kind of tragedy is explored, though it seems there to be most exactly defined. It is not to say that *Troilus* is Shakespeare's most important play.

But the definition there is the definition in some
sense of all the tragedies ; it includes the devasta-
tion of reason as well as sensation, and it affords a
point from which the contrasted explorations of
Milton and Shakespeare may be seen. Since Milton
determined to make reason an element in the quality
of his poem, he had to transmute Troilus's revolt
into a revolt against an apprehended moral Good.
He had to involve Reason, therefore he had to be
moral, but it is Reason and not conduct which is the
daystar, moon, and heavenly sun of his verse. In
the play there was no need for the Trojan to know
or to believe that Cressida, and the kind of love
which moved Cressida, were in accord with Reason
in its most exalted mood. He had to do with partial,
not universal, life. But Satan knows that the Love
which created him was in such accord, and so do
Adam and Eve. They certainly are not in revolt
against a new fact, but against an old fact newly
and unwisely apprehended. They do not seem to
themselves to have lost what they had, only not to
have what they desire to have. Adam himself is the
least guilty of the three; his fault lies in a too-foolish
and too-natural preference of Eve to an unknown
and (as he fears) desolate future. But Reason in
the Miltonic sense demands that he shall remain
faithful to the clear truth of his own identity as
he knows it, subordinated to perfection, not to be
guided or governed even by a passionately loved
imperfection. It was not enough that Satan should
fall in the all but undefinable choice of his first decision ; there must be a warmer and more intense
parallel to that choice in the Paradisal humanities.

Beauty in her incarnation is to become a temptation; it is exactly not truth, and is known not to be truth. All the lovely descriptions of Eve enhance the fact; all the stern assertions of the lordship of Adam emphasize the conflict. He *knows*, and she tempts; Beauty, raised to a single, exquisite, and imperative power, tempts mortal truth to deny itself in action.

Perhaps, in this sense, the nearest Miltonic poet to Milton was Patmore; in fact, Patmore might be described as Milton without Satan. He and Hardy confront each other in opposing singularities. His verse, allowing for its own peculiar genius, comes more near than that of any other English poet to the Miltonic scope and splendour; and his God, more easily perhaps than Milton's, might be conceived to be the originator of the heaven of which he is equally the climax. Patmore's poetry, including from the beginning the hypothesis of Deity, proceeded to enlarge the humanity, and decrease the assumption in that hypothesis; he identified his Godhead with a state of perfect joy, and he made that joy convincing, and explored its nature continually throughout his work. He explored also, sometimes philosophically, sometimes dramatically, man's capacities for refusing, evading, or misbelieving that joy, and the varying obediences and dominations which it demands. It seems that he is more easily believed than Milton; he is not popular, but he is not generally regarded as inhuman. Yet one would have thought that 'the white-cold virgin snow' of some of the *Odes* would have been more remote from recognition than even the bright-harnessed company or the angelic 'Maia's son'. He gave, however, no hostages to fortune in the shape of Satan, and his fortune, therefore, has not been able to identify his poetry almost entirely with Satan. He did not even go as far as Troilus, or rather his way branched off before Troilus was reached. In the *Victories of Love*, Frederick Graham does not win Honoria, but as Honoria was never believed to be his, it is only an intense possibility and not a fact of identity which is denied. Reason in Patmore was so exalted that his genius never presented a figure warring against it or finding it utterly in schism. It is just possible that this has militated a little against his fame; an integrity so absolute leaves him a little alienated from the most of scrabbling humanity. It is, no doubt, our fault, as the result is our misfortune.

Reason then in Hardy and Patmore and Milton controlled all things, although Milton's Reason included extremes which the poetry of the others did not. As a result Milton's very rebels had to reason at least as far as they could. Satan explores his knowledge of himself deliberately; Adam and Eve find the best reasons possible for their action. The manner of the verbal style of *Paradise Lost* is reasonable; it proceeds by inflexible statements raised to infinite power by their passion. The geometric laws of the universe are united with the poetic song of the universe, as if the Wordsworthian Arab's stone and shell had become one complex mystery of utterance. The soul knows how she felt, in the thrilling descriptions, and what she felt, in the thrilling definitions, and both in great moments of union. She knows herself 'warring in heaven against heaven's matchless king'; she knows herself again 'exhausted, spiritless, afflicted, fallen'. She feels against her the wall of heaven 'returning whence it rolled'; again she feels the progress of Messias through unrevolting chaos. She feels the soft hand, the rash hand, the liberal hand, the hand in hand of the last lingering departure. All are facts of a double category, and she knows them with the same exactitude with which they are there new-created.

But if she knows them in Shakespeare also, it is in a very different way, for more even than Milton did Shakespeare confine his meaning within—I do not say *to*—his dramatic style. We know the kind of drama Milton would have written had he written plays; *Comus* and the draft of the dramatic *Paradise* are there to prove it. We can hardly deduce from *Venus and Adonis*, *Lucrece*, and the *Sonnets*, the kind of epic poem that Shakespeare would have written, though it would be a fascinating game to discuss it. Had it followed the same lines as his actual development did, we might have had an epic which was itself less doctrinal and presented its protagonist as more passive than Milton's. The interweaving achievements of those two poets are complementary and contrasted at once. Satan and Eve and Adam deny their perceptions; they choose to know otherwise than in the duty and delight of love. But Troilus and Othello are forced or deceived into perceiving a change in identity of love, and even Lear, though he betrays himself, does so in the haste of natural anger and the play does not encourage us to inquire at what point in his past history his earlier moral delinquency lay. Even Macbeth is persuaded into temptation by the promise of an apparent good fulfilled; whereas Satan is enraged into temptation by the appearance of an unexpected good in the begetting of Messias. He has, and was meant to have, less excuse even than Macbeth.

The style of Shakespeare therefore, concentrated to express a schism in identity, and in the knowledge of identity, developed in itself a greater and greater concentration of perception. It would be rash to say that his style is much more concentrated than Milton's. But the concentrations in Milton are generally of things that agree; in Shakespeare they are often of things that differ. 'He for God only; she for God in him', is an example of the first; 'Nothing at all, unless that this were she', of the second. The extreme point of Satan,

> All good to me is lost;
> Evil, be thou my good,

is still aware of the significance which Macbeth has lost and of 'the odds' which had abandoned Cleopatra.

In another age an attempt was made to unite, as it were, those two great powers of poetry. It was made on a much lower level, and it—not unnaturally —failed. But the heroic drama of the Restoration seems to have tried to maintain (however unconsciously) the rational awareness of Milton containing the schism in reason of Shakespeare. Passion, in consequence, became the passions ; reason became argument; poetry too often became rhetoric and even rant. The absurd—but magnificently absurd —line of Dryden,

The Moors have heaven, and me, to assist their cause,

fails no doubt because (to us, at any rate, and perhaps we *are* better judges than Dryden) it lacks the final touch of poetic energy. It remains therefore an anti-rational statement expressed in terms which belong to clear reason. The spirits of the characters have to be extreme, but then Dryden and his like disapproved of extremity and withdrew from it in their style; when they presented it therefore they had to do so in terms of the balance of which they did approve. Their phrases are too lucid and too long ; yet they are not in their meaning wilder than some of Shakespeare's. Macbeth's invocation of utter destruction cannot be outgone by any heroic playwright.

It is not—in spite of Wordsworth's prose—the primal duty of poetry directly to encourage, exhort, or console. That it may do by the way, if we choose to take it so ; but to make of it the chief purpose is to turn poetry into a compensation for something lacked or lost, and, valuable as compensations are, poetry is too great for such a secondary business. The testimony which two great poets bore, in their poetry, to its nature, teaches us that. Marlowe told us that we beheld in it the highest reaches of human wit ; Wordsworth that forms and substances existed in it as if in their proper home ; it is not improper to add the lines of Milton when he believed that in poetry all mists were dispersed and things invisible to mortal sight made clear. If then we are to approach it properly, we must be willing to believe that its operations in its own world go far beyond our operations in ours. It is not by the morals we draw from it or the maxims it inculcates or the

melodies it releases that we shall be encouraged or
consoled. We must enter into its own world. But in
that world we may perhaps behold not merely our
present but our future capacities, and begin to recognize forms and substances not yet clearly known.
Reaches beyond our present paltry wits are mirrored
there ; and of those reaches one perhaps may hold
within it our own perpetual concern with truth and
beauty. It seems to be in the nature of man that
he should desire both ; that he should hunger to
find out real and final identities—of ideas or emotions or persons—and believe that such discoveries
will be consistent with joy. It is this composure
and ennobling harmony that he seeks in his own
spirit. He argues with himself like Pope, or he
escapes into convolutions of loveliness like Spenser,
but the highest reaches of his wit are not there.
He finds sometimes in art or religion or love a
music like the Nightingale's or a perpetual recol-
lection of union like the Urn ; but such forms and
substances, wonderful as they are, demand that he
shall forget something; and if ignored exactitude returns, the transmuted but timorous beauty perishes
like Lamia before the eyes of Apollonius. Or by
some terrible fact or persuasive deception—and who
in his moment can decide any more than Othello
whether the Iago of apparent exterior truthfulness
is indeed honest or not?—he is distracted in his
belief in both truth and beauty. The identities of
his life lose their nature, and either in a Satanic
decision or a Lear-like madness he feels himself
impaired. It is no less agony that it is an agony
which his own sin or folly has invited, as hell was no

less hell because Satan chose it and the storm on the
heath no less tempestuous because Lear had thrust
himself in the way of it. So far indeed—in their
lesser degree— the reaches of our wit usually go ;
these forms and substances are familiar enough.
But the great poets have gone farther. Milton for
a second—even *Paradise Lost* contemplated under
the heaven which itself creates is but a second—held
the universe still and silent (but for its responsive
joy) in the circumfusing light of sublime rapture,
saving only those forms who demanded of heaven
another gift and exactly received what they demanded ; through the midst of that whole universe
the self-abandoning spirit, the Messias of all vision,
moves celebrated to his eternal repose, out of which
he has yet never been. In that union of the supreme
heavenly climax with the Filial Godhead which is
the promised seed of human passion for truth and
beauty, the Third Person of the Christian Trinity
does not appear ; the Holy Spirit is omitted from
the Miltonic mythology. Or would be, if the poem
itself were not the Spirit ; it is in the revelation of
the poem that all things, even the Divine Persons,
exist, and it was the Spirit that was invoked to be
the poem. Within or without the meaning of Christian dogma, it assented; it came, and the poem grew
translucent and illustrious with its light. Within or
without that meaning the union of truth and beauty
was not merely declared but communicated as experience, and to that experience we return as to a
world of forms and substances more awful and more
real than the phantoms of our own. But Shakespeare invoked no such aid, and discovered no such

reach of human wit. More generally human—
let us give the commentators that; in the company
of the poets what does it matter what folly any of
us write ?—than his all-but-equal, he stretched his
genius upon the yonder side of Reason. He destroyed intelligence, and outraged humanity, and
discerned creation alike without any beauty and
any identity but anarchical nothingness. In the
moment of such destruction he reunited what he
had destroyed. Without any asserted philosophical
hypothesis he changed his style and became new.

We do not and cannot know in what temper of
mind he wrote the last comedies; but, whatever
our private judgement may be, reflected from our
private experiences or hopes, it is at least certain
that there he defined identities as finally as ever
before. It is certain also that he created in the
Winter's Tale and the *Tempest* lovers who are blessed
in love, and old men blessed, though with less of
high passion, in forgiveness. To Imogen he gave a
sweet swift pardon, but natural beatitude surrounds
Florizel and Perdita in good fortune or misfortune,
and even their temporality is refused to Miranda
and Ferdinand. Those two exist for and in their
moment alone. The unities of dramatic concentration are so present—as they always should be but
rarely are—that all past and future may be felt in
the instant, but as the instant and not as themselves.
Truth and beauty, from whatever cause, are here
absolutely one in the perfection of Shakespeare's
style; itself as magical as the enchanted island, as
earthly as Caliban, as elemental as Ariel, as lovely
as Miranda. In a too rash fantasy the island itself

might seem to float for its permitted hour in its
ocean as the earth itself might seem to float in blue
space, and upon it the principles of human life, incarnated into forms, live and move and are harmo-
niously united in the composure of delight. But so
far a dream is our own dallying with the innocence
of love ; we may indulge but must not impose it.
We must not repose upon anything but the style—
the manner of diction and rhythm, the purpose
and dramatic meaning with which the diction and
rhythms were used.

The Fool in *Lear* (so Kent told us) had

> laboured to outjest
> His heart-struck injuries.

That jesting seems to be prolonged into the joy of
the comedies, where our heart-struck injuries are
saved from striking to the very bottom of the heart,
as if by the equally prolonged power of

> the clearest gods who make them honour
> Of men's impossibilities.

It is the only triumph we may agree that we have
in Shakespeare—the triumph of his style, and the
abolition of the nightmare Life-in-Death by a sound
that is 'now like all instruments, Now like a lonely
flute'.

The high poetry of our greatest poet contained
certainly, if Marlowe was right, the very highest
reaches of our human wit. We have made a complex experience of him, and some new Augustan
coolness may have to rebuke the romantic heat. But
meanwhile we have to decide for ourselves whether
that heat is fever or healthy ardour; whether that

union of beauty and truth in poetry mirrors states of being our Trojan or Danish or Moorish spirits may at last attain ; whether it is indeed just to say that in this mode of experience which we call the world there are at least two great realities, Shakespeare and Death.

Lightning Source UK Ltd.
Milton Keynes UK
24 November 2009

146689UK00001B/45/A